Robert M. Buermann

WITHDRAWN

BURIED TREASURE

Model showing how the Stonehenge uprights may have been raised into position.
Author is on the right.

BURIED
TREASURE

Paul Johnstone

WITH 67 PLATES
AND A FRONTISPIECE

PHOENIX HOUSE LTD
LONDON

To N

Printed in Great Britain
in 11/13 point Monotype Garamond by
C. Tinling & Co. Ltd., Liverpool, London, and Prescot,
for Phoenix House Ltd, 38 William IV Street,
Charing Cross, W.C.2.

First published 1957

Contents

Illustrations

Model showing how the Stonehenge uprights may have been raised *frontis.*

Foreword

This book is the story of a series of television programmes, whose earliest beginnings date back to 1 October 1952. On that day I joined the BBC Television Service and was told that in three weeks' time I had to make a programme out of a challenge match between a museum and a panel of experts. This is not the place for a history of 'Animal, Vegetable, Mineral?' but it turned out that the programme's eventual success had given me and the chairman, Dr Glyn Daniel of St John's College, Cambridge, the same idea. We both wanted to move on from dealing with a single object at a time to a full television treatment of an archaeological subject.

The first two that we tackled were the centenary of Sir Flinders Petrie and the work of the Science Laboratory of the British Museum. Neither programme was a complete failure, but I think, looking back, that their main virtue was the large amount which they taught us. In June 1954 a programme about Tollund Man established 'Buried Treasure' as a successful series. The eleven programmes after that make up the balance of this book.

In turning the story of them into a book various changes became inevitable. Pictures that make a point in an instant often require many words in their place. Equally it has been possible to fill in various gaps which the inexorable half-hour of television planning previously forced on us. But the main change is in the order. Many things affected the order of the television series, from programme schedules to the availability of people and dates of excavations. Here I have simply put them in chronological order as subjects, which ideally we should have liked for the series.

My thanks are due to many people for their help with the series and so with this book; Mr McGivern, Deputy Director of Television Broadcasting, Mrs Adams, and Mr Miall, Head of Television Talks, for their encouragement, the Film, Studio, and Special Effects departments of the BBC, Museum officials, and innumerable others.

Then in the course of producing these programmes, I have had a first-hand introduction to their subject matter from some of the best-qualified archaeologists in Europe. I have above all had the constant help and advice of Glyn Daniel. To all of them I give my best thanks for a much-appreciated privilege which few other laymen can have had.

I am also extremely grateful to Sir Mortimer Wheeler, Dr Oakley, Dr Weiner, Professor Seán Ó Ríordáin, Professor Evans, Mr Burkitt and Dr Kenyon for their comments and corrections on various chapters in this book though of course the responsibility for any mistakes is mine. But for all their help I must make it quite clear that I do not write in any sense as an archaeologist. I am just a layman who has heard and read much of interest during these programmes.

Working on them made me turn to the sources quoted in the bibliography, the works of archaeologists who can write with authority. I gained much pleasure thereby and I hope this book may encourage others to do the same.

* * *

Permission to use photographs has kindly been given to me by the Director of the British Museum (Natural History) (Plates 2 and 5), Professor Ó Riórdaín (Plate 29), Miss Sally Kistruck (Plate 35), Aerofilms Ltd (Plates 37 and 61), Mr R. J. C. Atkinson (Plates 38 and 39), and the *Salisbury Journal* (Plate 32). The BBC have also allowed me to use many stills from films specially taken for the 'Buried Treasure' series.

CHAPTER I

PILTDOWN MAN

ONE AFTERNOON, in May 1955, I found myself involved in an important discussion. Five of us were standing round a film camera in the drive of Barkham Manor in Sussex. The camera was focused on a dried-out puddle. The discussion was whether the stones round the edge of the puddle would look like gravel on the television screen. This unlikely activity was a result of several million British viewers' willingness to enjoy archaeological programmes. The gravel, unpromising as it might seem visually, was an important link in the story which I was then working on.

For weeks previously, I had been reading all the information I could find and discussing the programme with Dr Oakley, of the British Museum of Natural History. The relevant facts I had gathered in this way seemed to be these.

In late November 1912 a plump Sussex solicitor found that his hobby had brought him national fame. His name was Charles Dawson. His feat was to have found valuable evidence of man's early origins. At that time this was a comparatively new way to achieve distinction in the scientific world.

It was only a little over sixty years since Boucher de Perthes, a French customs official, had first put forward a convincing case for the antiquity of man with his discovery of some crude flint tools in the ancient gravels of the River Somme. Until then the vast majority of people would happily have accepted some such date as Archbishop Ussher's seventeenth century suggestion, 4004 B.C., for the Creation. But as the scientific interest of the nineteenth century replaced the Romantic attitude to the past of the eighteenth century and the neglect of earlier periods, startling new ideas began to appear. Imagined golden ages yielded to the facts of geology. Once the slow accumulation of the strata of the earth was properly appreciated, a truer perspective of the vast reaches of the past became possible. After the work of T. H. Huxley and Darwin, a large part of scientific opinion was prepared to accept the descent of man from ape-like ancestors.

It is hard now to remember, when we so casually take for granted man's long, slow emergence to humanity, that as recently as fifty years ago it was a new and gripping idea. All that was needed was concrete evidence to support it. Remains of Neanderthal and Cro-Magnon man had been found during the nineteenth century but their exact significance was not properly understood. Then in 1892 Dubois found part of a skull-cap, a femur, and two doubtful teeth of a strange, ape-like creature now known as Java man.

In 1907 Otto Schoentensack's year-in, year-out watch on the Mauer sand quarry was rewarded by the finding of the jaw of Heidelberg man. Now in 1912 the sharp eyes of the amateur archaeologist from Lewes, whose duties as a solicitor took him regularly to Barkham Manor in the village of Piltdown, had found, amongst the iron-stained flints of the gravel-bed alongside its drive, the most important pieces of evidence yet.

His friend, Arthur Smith-Woodward, Keeper of the Department of Geology at the British Museum, first publicly summed up this evidence at a hushed and excited meeting of the Geological Society in London. There were nine pieces of dark brown, unusually thick, human skull-bone and part of a lower jaw with two molars still in place. With them had appeared a number of flints so crudely chipped that it was doubtful whether they were of human workmanship, others also crude but patently of human manufacture, and remains of numerous animals, including hippopotamus, deer, beaver, mastodon, and rhinoceros. Considering the ancient geological level in which they had been found, these flints and fossils all seemed to make a convincing case for the existence of a primitive ape-man in England between 500,000 and a million years ago.

The discovery was excitedly described as epoch-making. Dawson's perception was saluted by the title *Eoanthropus dawsonii*, Dawson's dawn man, which was given to the new ancestor of the human race. Re-written history books had to find a place for Piltdown man.

But even at that very first meeting there were a number of sceptics. However much the human skull and ape-like jaw appeared to fulfil Darwin's prediction of an early apeman, they were difficult to accept anatomically as coming from the same creature.

Thereafter, for the next three years, the new famous patch of Piltdown gravel and the nearby countryside yielded a barrage of further evidence to confound these sceptics. First came a canine tooth. This was vital because much argument had centred on the wear likely to be caused to ape-like teeth by a freely moving human jaw. It confirmed almost exactly Smith-Woodward's prediction of its probable shape.

Then there was a remarkable slab of fossil elephant bone, carved at one end to a point, the earliest known bone tool.

Finally, and most conclusively, in 1915 parts of the skull and a molar of another creature of the same type were found about two miles away at a site that has never been identified. Dawson died in 1916, so the war prevented his seeing the full impact of this last discovery on the sceptics.

You could argue that the skull and jaw might belong to two different creatures, a fossil man and a fossil ape, which had come together by chance, as long as there was only one example of them close together. When another example of the same combination was found two miles away, it was stretching belief too far to say that this was coincidence also.

However, as the years passed, Piltdown man, though generally accepted, began to appear more and more odd. The trouble was the combination of human skull and ape-like jaw. All the other new discoveries that were made through the years had the opposite combination, an ape-like skull and a more human jaw.

The belief that Piltdown man was an odd, ancient freak, a sideline which had died out about 500,000 years ago and left no other traces, was finally destroyed by Dr K. Oakley in 1949. Through a fluorine test he showed that the skull and jaw could not be more than 50,000 years old at the most.

Fluorine is a substance present in the soil, which is gradually absorbed by any bones lying there. Chemically, it is possible to measure the amount in a bone. Different soils from different sites contain varying amounts of fluorine, but it is obviously possible to tell from the amount in two bones from the same site how long they have been there as compared to each other. In this case the skull, jaw, and hippopotamus specimens proved to have a far smaller content of fluorine than the elephant tooth, which contained the amount to be expected if the elephant had lived some 500,000 years ago.

Hippopotamus became extinct in Britain before 50,000 B.C. so as the skull had the same very small quantity of fluorine as the hippopotamus tooth, that now put Piltdown man somewhere in the latter part of the Ice Age.

However, if he was an oddity dated to 500,000 years ago, he was nonsense only 50,000 years old with no known ancestors or descendants. Nor were the people who thought the skull and jaw belonged to two different creatures much helped, since it was impossible to believe in the existence of a fossil ape in Britain at the end of the Ice Age.

The explanation first occurred to Dr Weiner, Reader in Physical Anthropology at Oxford. He was driving back there one evening after a meeting in London at which discussion of Piltdown man had cropped up, when it struck him that the only really strong evidence to link the jaw and brain-case was the peculiar flat wear of the teeth, supposedly caused by a freely moving, human-like jaw. A possibility that would explain all the contradictions was that part of a modern ape's jaw had been deliberately placed with the more ancient pieces of skull, with the teeth ground down to hide its modernity and to give Piltdown man his peculiar intermediate character.

The idea was startling, to say the least, but Dr Weiner's examination of the casts of the specimens at Oxford the next morning, far from disposing of it, hurried him on to further enquiries. Not only was the flat wear of the teeth quite extraordinary, but all the other tell-fale features that might have revealed an attempt to pass off a modern jaw as a fossil were missing, like the condyle or bony knob where the jaw joins the skull, and the chin region. You can see for yourself in Plate 3 that this unnatural flat wear of the Piltdown molars, as compared with ordinary human molars shown alongside, is apparent even to the naked eye, while the exposure of the little flat triangles of dentine in the enamel covering is quite unlike anything known in nature.

In fact, Dr Weiner was able, by filing down a chimpanzee's molars and staining them with permanganate, to produce specimens almost identical with the Piltdown molars and, what is more, he assures me that it was an operation that required neither great manual dexterity nor special dental knowledge.

The subsequent inquiries were intensive and detailed and used every scientific method and device that had any relevance. The conclusion is now well known and almost universally accepted—that Piltdown man was one of the most successful frauds in the history of science.

For the details of the enquiry, you must read the account of Dr K. P. Oakley and the others concerned in the Bulletin of the British Museum, Natural History (vol. 2, no. 3, 1953) and Dr Weiner's *The Piltdown Forgery*.

I have only outlined here the story in the form in which I thought we should present it on television. It was one of the most extraordinary archaeological events of the age, and so we could hardly neglect it in a series devoted to archaeology. The problem was how it should be done.

There were basically two possible methods. You could study the known facts, dramatize them, and give actors the job of re-creating the characters, motives, and activities of Dawson, Smith-Woodward, and the others. Or you could get someone who knew the facts to tell the story, illustrating it where relevant with material or pictorial evidence. By inclination and training, I favoured the second, and in one form or another this documentary method has been used in all the Buried Treasure programmes.

The Piltdown story presented no great difficulties as a subject. Photographs or paintings existed of all the main characters, we could film the sites, and, most important of all, the skull, jaw, and other evidence could be shown in great detail and in a way that made the order of events as clear as possible.

The recent part, the revelation of the fraud, was easier still. Most of the methods used could be filmed at the Natural History museum or even demonstrated in the studio. It made a fascinating detective story.

I cannot say that I actually smelt burning horn, as Dr Oakley and Mr Parsons of the Geological Department did when they first drilled the jaw, but there was no doubt about the difference between the sample drillings from it and the skull. Enlarged photographically, the skull shavings were seen as the fine dust one would expect of fossil bones. The jaw, on the other hand, produced fine strips of peeling just as fresh bone would.

Other chemical tests, such as the measurement of the nitrogen content, confirmed this difference between the skull and jaw. They could not possibly have come from the same creature, while the jaw showed every sign of modernity.

The famous solitary canine tooth yielded its secrets. A fresh tooth is very difficult to stain, so for this the forger almost certainly used vandyke brown paint. The scratches made when the crown of the tooth was ground down are clearly visible when magnified, and an X-ray shows that when the filing exposed the pulp cavity in the centre of the tooth, this was plugged with a piece of plastic material. As Dr Oakley remarked, fossil apes don't usually have their teeth stopped!

The next demonstration was visually very effective. Dr Oakley applied some dilute hydrochloric acid to one of Piltdown man's supposed flint tools, whose reddish brown colour matched that of the Piltdown gravel. After a few moments he rubbed it off, leaving a distinct yellowish-whitish patch where the brown iron staining had come away. When the same process was tried on one of the naturally iron-stained flints from the Piltdown gravel, nothing happened at all. In fact, Piltdown man's tools were probably whitish wasters, that is, pieces discarded by flint knappers in late prehistoric times, from the nearby Sussex Downs, stained by the forger to match the prevailing iron-stained brown of the other Piltdown finds.

Another method of staining tried was the dipping of some of the specimens in a solution of a chromium compound, probably bichromate. Dawson told Smith-Woodward he had done this to the skull fragments in the mistaken impression it would harden them, but this hardly explains why traces of chromium should be found on the jaw and one of the flints.

The large slab of fossilized elephant bone proved as fraudulent as the canine. It is impossible to match the marks on it by carving fresh bone with a sharpened flint. You can saw or scrape, but to whittle it in that way you must use a metal knife and choose a fossil bone of chalk-like consistency.

For the animal specimens which had so conveniently dated Piltdown man, the forger had collected specimens from all over the place.

The hippopotamus molar turned out, for instance, to have the low fluorine and low organic content typical of the many hippopotamus molars found in caves in the Mediterranean islands like Malta. The only trouble is that they are a creamy white in colour, but the author of the hoax had dealt with that as he had done with the flint tools. They were stained the prevailing Piltdown brown.

The Piltdown elephant tooth came from even further away. This was shown by the most fascinating test of all. First the Piltdown jaw was placed in a lead casket, inside which a geiger counter picked up the radiations from it. The results were shown on a dial with a moving pointer. As one would expect from fresh bone from English soil, it was scarcely radio-active at all, and the pointer only clicked round two or three times in a minute.

Then the Piltdown elephant tooth was put in the cabinet in its place. As soon as the apparatus was switched on the pointer fairly clattered round the dial, at the rate of something like 200 counts a minute.

An elephant tooth from Ichkeul in Tunisia gave an almost identical result. Ichkeul is a well-known site that has produced many fossil remains, all with this characteristic high radio-activity. No other elephant remains from this early period, from other parts of the world, are nearly as radio-active. It seems very likely, therefore, that the Piltdown elephant tooth came from North Africa, before it was planted to give a fraudulent date to *Eoanthropus dawsonii*.

Finally, even the skull, which many had thought at least had been genuinely found there before the faked jaw was added, was shown to have been doctored.

While the methods of the forgery have been so brilliantly revealed, it is much more difficult to see why it was done and by whom. The findings of Weiner and Oakley seem to point irrevocably to Dawson. Yet, psychologically, it seems to me as a layman that his behaviour is difficult to explain consistently. If he was the villain from the start he must have acted with an extraordinary mixture of simple stupidity and brilliant cunning.

Of the eoliths, the flints so crudely chipped that it is doubtful that they were the work of man, Weiner says: 'The forger's intention may have gone slightly astray in not attaining the most ancient heritage possible for his brain-child', yet Dawson himself argued against the earlier date suggested for 'Eoanthropus'. If that is not a subtle piece of double bluff, it must at least have been a swift and calculating adaptation to circumstances. Is that consistent with what Weiner calls 'the glaring miscalculation or oversight' in using a chromium compound to assist the iron-staining of the flint tools, or the rashness in making the elephant bone tool so improbable?

Perhaps Dawson was duped. Perhaps he was duped by someone who planted the first specimens and then blackmailed him into going on with the deception. Perhaps it was all a joke, that went too far to stop.

These were theories that there was not time to discuss in the programme. Perhaps one day someone will come forward and reveal beyond discussion the motives of the forger. That too would make a programme which I should look forward to producing.

CHAPTER II

THE ALTERNATIVE TO PILTDOWN

——————

A COMMON REACTION amongst laymen after the revelation of the Piltdown fraud was to suspect all the rest of pre-history. In fact the Piltdown enquiry, by developing many new methods, has been a benefactor to science and increased both the means available for the study of fossils and primitive man and current knowledge of them.

I thought therefore that any programme on Piltdown must end on a positive note. Having shown how the fraud was revealed, we must then put the other side, what had in fact been confirmed of the early history of man.

Dr Weiner did this with copies of eight skulls on a specially designed stand. Each skull was on a shelf labelled with its name and date. The shelves were side by side but rose above one another according to age. Dr Weiner began his story, which I have expanded here with information he and Dr Oakley gave me at other times, with the skull on the lowest shelf, that of *Proconsul*.

About twenty million years ago, he explained, a type of early ape in East Africa had left the trees and started living mainly on the ground. A skull of one has been found and the species has been given the name *Proconsul*. They could climb trees still, but spent much time peering over the tall grasses in the open. In these circumstances their feet would be inclined to lose their grasping power, as they walked more and more upright, and their hands, free from having to swing from branch to branch, to become less specialized and more skilful.

Professor Carleton Coon has said that if the finest contemporary engineers were to sit down for weeks to design a perfect tool for grasping and fine manipulation, they could come out with nothing better than the human hand. It was an upright posture that enabled man's hands to develop in this way, and it was man's skilful hands that enabled him to make tools.

'Man is a tool-making animal', said Benjamin Franklin. The accent should be on the 'making'. The North American solitary burrowing wasp uses a pebble as a hammer to hide the surface traces of its burrow. The Cactospiza, a finch from the Galapagos Islands, uses a cactus spine to dig out insects from the cracks in the branch of a tree. A southern sea-otter off the coast of California has been seen to bring to the surface, together with a small slab of rock, a shellfish whose delicate flesh is guarded by a very hard shell. Turning on its back, the otter lays the slab of rock on its chest and, holding the shellfish in both paws, bangs it against the slab until it is cracked. Sultan, a male chimpanzee, fitted a small bamboo cane into a larger one to make a stick long enough to get hold of a bunch of bananas which was too far away for one cane alone to reach.

All these examples are quoted by Doctor K. P. Oakley in his fascinating chapter 'Skill as a human possession' in the *History of Technology*. But all these actions, he explains, are the result of instinct, trial and error, or for a visible reward. Only man can see the point of making an object for use in an imagined situation.

A chimpanzee will pull a loose board from a box to use as a stick, but if the boards of the box are nailed together to present an unbroken surface, he will not see a number of possible sticks in it, even though he is strong enough to break up the box and his need for a stick is urgent.

Man, on the other hand, will visualize a tool which he needs in a shapeless lump of stone, and work on it until it is in the form which he imagined. This process is called conceptual thought.

Roughly summarized, the physical and mental features which are necessary before conceptual thought becomes possible are an opposable thumb, which makes it possible to pick up objects between finger and thumb instead of just in a paw, stereoscopic and colour vision, an erect posture so that close attention can be paid to any point over a wide field of vision, and a sufficiently fine and well-developed brain and nervous system to co-ordinate delicate impulses from hand and eye, store them up as memories, and profit from them as experience.

Monkeys have an opposable thumb and stereoscopic and colour vision. It has even been reported that chimpanzees can learn to co-ordinate hand and eye sufficiently to thread a needle. The trouble is that the concentration they can give to anything is very fleeting, and their limited ability to think in 'images' restricts their mental development.

It took a vast period of time, though, both before and after *Proconsul*, before man and his ancestors reached the tool-making stage and had what Aristotle called 'the conception of the result to be produced before its realization in the material'.

Man is classified amongst the living beings of the world as a primate.
The earliest primates were the *Prosimii*, who evolved from tiny, insect-
eating creatures like those who left traces of their remains in the 100-
million-year-old Cretaceous rocks of North America. With sub-tropical
conditions, the *Prosimii* spread across most parts of the world. Like their
modern survivors, tree-shrews, lemurs, and tarsiers, they probably lived
mainly on fruit and insects. This diet, and the need to take shelter in trees,
developed the grasping and plucking powers of their fore limbs at the
expense of their teeth and sense of smell. Sight too was important in this
life amongst the trees, so the eyes, which at first were separated by a snout,
gradually shifted to a forward-facing position. When the eyes are close
enough together for both to focus on the same near point, the brain
receives a stereoscopic picture, that is, one having depth and solidity.
The difficulty you have in judging distances with one eye covered is a
common experience. Such a handicap would have been fatal in a life spent
swinging from branch to branch.

Then watch the difference between a dog or a hedgehog finding a
strange object, and a monkey. A dog or a hedgehog will sniff it. A monkey
will finger it, while examining it. The development of this co-ordination
between hand and eye eventually made possible man's skilled tool-making.

But first there had to come a development of the intelligence. Living in
trees had produced powers of seeing and holding. Now a return to the
ground, keeping these powers, developed intelligence and curiosity.

Over many millions of years the ancestors of monkeys, apes, and men
had evolved from those *Prosimii* who had grown in size and complexity
of brain. Now a certain group of these ancestors, about 20 million years
ago, left the trees and started living mainly on the ground. *Proconsul* is so
important because the surviving skull gives a great deal of information
about a species that was probably not very different from these ancestors
of us and the great apes.

Proconsul and our ancestors, like monkeys, were undoubtedly both
active and intensely curious. Walking or sitting on open ground, with
hands free to handle objects, they would soon do so first out of curiosity
then for a purpose. Baboons who live in the open sometimes use pebbles
to kill scorpions and at other times, if chased, will scamper up a hill-side
and roll boulders down on their pursuers.

Another result of living away from forests would be a more varied diet.
Anatomically we ought to be vegetarians. We have the long gut usually
associated with a vegetable diet and lack the teeth of flesh-eaters. But
when our ancestors left the trees, hunger must have driven them to eat
meat. Baboons raid African farms, and prey on poultry and even lambs. A

report from Zululand describes a troop of them surrounding an antelope, and at a given signal closing in and tearing it to pieces.

To store the same amount of energy a flesh-eater needs a smaller quantity of food than a vegetarian. Instead of spending their day continuously eating fruit and berries, man's ancestors must have given most of their time to hunting, which encouraged interdependence and group activity.

At first planned use of tools would have been beyond them, but from the spur of the hazardous life in the open, by about a million years ago, their brains had probably become sufficiently complex to achieve this.

This is a summary of some of the current views on evolution, which I should have liked Dr Weiner to have discussed at length in the programme. As it was, no traces of early man survive from this time, so he soon moved on to his second piece of evidence, an advanced type of ape called *Australopithecus*, remains of which have been found in South Africa. This small creature, about four foot high and fifty pounds in weight, was probably a sideline that died out, though it had the same ancestors as man. Its canine teeth were practically as small as man's, its brain was larger than an ape's, and its posture a good deal more upright. Animal bones, egg and crab shells, and baboon skulls that may have been artificially pierced, have been found with its remains in the caves at Taungs, Bechuanaland. In one of the Makapan caves in the Transvaal, a number of antelope limb-bones have been discovered deliberately smashed open, but without any tools. Dr Dart, the well-known South African anthropologist, believes that *Australopithecus* did this, though other people think hyenas may have been responsible.

It looks then as though *Australopithecus* lived in open country, hiding in caves and crannies, and probably using stones and sticks and bones to protect himself and kill small animals for food.

Tools have been found that probably date from this period, but not with any remains of their users. The earliest tools are difficult to distinguish because for a long time any convenient, sharp-edged stone had been used remove the skin from a hunted animal. Then some more intelligent individual saw that you could get a fresh, sharp edge by deliberately breaking a pebble, and tool-making had begun.

These earliest examples come from the Kafu valley in Uganda, from Kanam in Kenya, and elsewhere in Africa. They consist of pebbles flaked to produce a cutting edge and are sufficiently standard in form to be accepted as deliberately made.

Dr Weiner next turned to a copy of the skull of the oldest known fossil man. No tools at all were found with *Pithecanthropus robustus*, Java man, whose remains are probably 500,000 to 600,000 years old. Nor did any come to light with the rather later, but similar, Heidelberg man, the finding of whose jaw in 1907 probably helped to inspire the Piltdown forger. But both show considerably more human characteristics than *Australopithecus*. The teeth and jaw, though still keeping some ape-like characteristics, are more human, the brain is larger, and they stood fully erect.

The earliest known fossil man who definitely made tools is Pekin man. Thousands of artificially broken stones, many of a kind foreign to the site, have been found in the caves at Choukoutien in China with his remains. Many are so crude that had they been found on their own they would hardly have been accepted as tools.

Apparently he collected stones from a nearby river bed and cliffs and brought them to his cave, where he broke them up by using a stone slab or large bone as an anvil and striking them with a hammerstone.

It is also known that he was a successful hunter, from the quantity of butchered animal remains, was possibly a cannibal, could make fire, and was usually right-handed. His most pleasing characteristic was that he had some artistic feelings. Crystals of quartz, that presumably attracted him by their shape and appearance, had been brought many miles to his cave for no other useful purpose.

This characteristic can also be seen in the great Acheulian culture, which between 300,000 and 400,000 B.C. began to spread from Africa to Europe and South Asia, as man and tool-making had done in the first place.

Archaeologists use the word culture in a specific sense. It is the name given to a way of life, including tool-making, that is found over an area or period of time. It is sometimes asked 'how can these cultures be defined so authoritatively when the early ones are just based on bits of chipped stone?' An answer can be found in the Acheulian culture (Pl. 5). Hand-axes typical of it from London, Kenya, Madras and the Cape are indistinguishable in form, whether made of flint, sandstone, quartz, or lava. The awkwardly named hand-axe was a roughly triangular piece of stone sharpened at the point, which was held in the hand and probably used as a hunter's knife, vital for cutting up the prey into pieces small enough to carry back to camp, for digging up grubs and roots, and cut-ing wood. Many show an artistic skill and finish that go well beyond necessity. In a recognizable form they are found over a fifth of the globe, and the type endured for over a hundred thousand years. This slowness in development was not because the brains of these primitive hunters were much inferior to those of the average person today. The only undoubted skull of an Acheulian hand-axe maker was found at Swanscombe near the River Thames in 1935 (a further piece of it was found in 1955). Though probably more than 100,000 years old, it is scarcely distinguishable in shape from some modern skulls.

The slowness came from the small numbers of the population, their lack of accumulated knowledge, and possibly also because language was still in a very elementary state. New ideas would be slow to come and circulate while language was mainly gabble and gesture.

The Stone Age hunter made an axe in a particular way because as a child, he had seen someone else do so. The standard type was not conceived at one go by any one person. It appeared as the result of exceptional persons in successive generations not only copying, but occasionally improving, the traditional model.

For the details of how the various cultures grew, blended, or disappeared at a gradually increasing rate, you must read Dr Oakley's *Man, the Toolmaker*, or L. S. B. Leakey's *Adam's Ancestors*. The succession of these cultures has a fine sonorous roll largely derived from the French sites which gave them their names—Tayacian, Abbevillian, Acheulian, Clactonian, Levalloisian, Mousterian, Micoquian and so on. I always think that Clactonian adds a note of almost Cockney cheek to this list. I have a vision of some primitive East Ender on a cheerful outing to the Essex coast blithely dropping a handful of tools in the mud and the name of Clacton into pre-history.

Of these Dr Weiner only considered for a moment the Mousterian culture because it was the product of Neanderthal man. Many views are held about him. Weiner's was that Neanderthal man was a specialized offshoot of mankind who preceded *Homo sapiens* in Europe. Though reminiscent in his great eyebrow-regions of our ape-like ancestors, he had a brain larger on average than those of modern man. He led a regular hunting and cave-dwelling life, cut up the animals he had killed and took portions back to the caves, and sometimes buried his dead ceremonially.

With the appearance of Cro-Magnon man in Europe about 50,000 B.C. Neanderthal man's day is done. Either he was ousted by or he developed into Cro-Magnon man. In cave-man fiction the hero seems always to be a handsome, clean-limbed Cro-Magnon. Inevitably he vanquishes the Neanderthal villain who, with his shaggy, beetling brows, shambles off to unmodified extinction.

So far we had illustrated Dr Weiner's telling of this story in the programme with a close-up of each appropriate skull. When he came to Cro-Magnon I put in a two-shot of a Cro-Magnon skull and Dr Glyn Daniel's head looking over the stand beside it. Weiner made the point with a nice touch of humour.

Cro-Magnon man is indistinguishable physically from modern Europeans. With his coming there is a dramatic quickening in the appearance of new tools and techniques. Some people argue that this may have been due to the invention of language and the better communication of ideas. It may even have been due to the spread of cooking. Eating raw meat takes a long time. Cooked food reduced the time spent eating and left more to evolve new skills.

Certainly there is a great elaboration in materials and the way they are used. Bone and ivory are worked as well as wood and stone. Spear-throwers and the bow reflect the first use of mechanical principles. Buttons, needles, and belt fasteners appear.

These made it possible to make clothes from skins, which in turn meant that man could survive the cold of the Ice Age, and inhabit the earth from the tropics to the arctic zones. There was even time to make purely decorative objects, like the head-dress of shells and stag's teeth buried with a Stone Age Warrior at Mentone. The Willendorf and Brassempouy figures show that women, too, had the same impulse. Already they were spending much time and trouble doing their hair.

This was a long way from an ape-like creature grabbing a bone in self-defence or killing a scorpion with a pebble. All was ready for the next step forward in Art and Religion and the most pleasing achievement of the Old Stone Age, at least from the point of view of subject matter for television.

CHAPTER III

THE DAWN OF ART

One morning, in September 1940, five boys set out rabbiting in occupied France. The place was the valley of the Vézère, whose wooded hill-sides look down on the little town of Montignac. The Germans were not far away across the border, the war had left many restrictions as well as uncertainties, but with the sun shining and the company of Robot, their dog, the day's prospects were cheerful.

These did not seem quite so good a few hours later when Robot had disappeared completely down the hole beneath a tree where a donkey had broken his leg some years back. However, Ravidat, the leader of the party, decided to try to get him out. Slipping and slithering, with stones and earth falling about his ears, he eventually got to his feet and found he was in a large oval chamber of a cave. This was surprising, but something even more remarkable was to come. A lighted match revealed that the cave was covered with an extraordinary procession of brightly painted animals.

By chance, he had become the first person for thousands of years to see the great show-place of Stone Age art, now known the world over as Lascaux. Much of the rest of surviving Stone Age art is hard to reach, faint, difficult to decipher, or worn away by the passage of time and sight-seers. The cave of Lascaux has none of these disadvantages. It is easy to get at. It is comfortable and simply lit, so that the visitor, while losing little of the sense of mystery, probably sees the paintings far better than prehistoric man did, with his flickering lamps and torches. The paintings are mostly done on a crystal skin that forms on this particular type of rock, so that the colours have the clear brilliance that might come from modern poster paints. The cave's position in the hill-side, which prevented the warm air outside condensing on the paintings in what has been described as a 'corrosive dew', has also helped to preserve them. It is a quite remarkable experience to see these bulls, horses, and deer, so clear, so bright, so easily recognizable, and yet so old and so utterly strange and mysterious. In this obscurity, Ravidat's discovery throws a sudden bright light. When I went to Lascaux in 1948 I heard much of this story from

Ravidat himself, who was a guide there then. But as Dr Daniel, and later the Abbé Breuil, explained to me it is easy to understand why people doubted for so long that Stone Age art was genuine.

By the latter part of the Old Stone Age, the 'Upper Palaeolithic' as it is called, from 30,000 to 10,000 years ago, man had achieved a varied and elaborate technique for making stone tools for various purposes. He worked bone as well as wood, and decorated his tools. For shelter, he relied on caves, overhanging rocks, or rough huts made of turf, brushwood, and even mammoth bones. Remains of these crude dwelling places used by mammoth hunters have been found in Central Europe and Russia. For clothes, as well as food, he relied on hunting and catching game.

For all this, he is infinitely remote to us and to civilization. His cunning at working stone and trapping animals was that of a savage, his possessions were limited to those he could carry with him, and his survival was dependent on the herds of game, which he followed in hungry need in family groups.

Then, suddenly, there comes this outburst of art, so vivid, so skilful, so sophisticated, that it is hard to believe its age. Its purpose may be strange, but the result is today as suitable for the nursery wall as Disney. But it took nearly seventy years to become accepted as a fact by modern man.

The first known example of Stone Age art was discovered in France only a little over a hundred years ago in 1834, when the biblical date for the Creation was generally accepted. It was therefore not surprising that the work in question, an engraving of two horses on a bone tool, was at first thought to be Celtic and to date from just before the Roman period. But this solitary piece was soon reinforced. With the spread of enthusiasm for discovering antiquities, other finds were made of similar bone and stone tools, decorated with engravings of animals and fishes, in undisturbed sites together with undoubtedly Stone Age objects. These Stone Age tools had already been studied quite considerably, and their association with bones of extinct animals and evidence of Ice Age conditions had established their great age. This antiquity was now admitted also for the decorated tools, or 'home art' as it was called, that were found with them.

But art, in the sense of pictures on a large scale, was a very different matter, as Marcellino de Sautuola was to discover. He was the Spanish archaeologist who was eventually led, disbelieving at first, by his five-year-old daughter's cries of 'los toros—the bulls, the bulls' to look at the roof of the great chamber of the cave of Altamira, and there see the famous cluster of red, ochre, and black bison, boar, and horses.

The remarkable nature of this find was admitted, but not its age. The figures were the work of cattle herders, or even the scribblings of Roman Legionaries. The world wondered and admired for a moment, and then forgot. Their true importance had to wait until the discovery of the paintings and caves round Les Eyzies in south-west France from 1895 onwards.

The calcareous rock through which the River Vézère has worn its valley is of a type and softness that easily forms caves. These were obviously known and used by Stone Age men and, unlike many more perishable remains, survive as an invaluable source of information about that period. The realization of this fact led to a tremendous outburst of cave-exploring in this district towards the end of the nineteenth century. The caves of La Mouthe, Font de Gaume, and Combarelles near Les Eyzies and Pair-non-Pair near Bordeaux became exciting sources of drawings and engravings for the small band of archaeologists who had realized their significance. What was perhaps most important was that the engravings at La Mouthe were only reached after clearing away undisturbed Stone Age deposits, authentic guardians and eloquent witness of their genuine age. In 1902 the evidence of La Mouthe was examined by a party from the conference held by the French Association for the Advancement of Science, which was meeting at Montauban. They were convinced. Cartailhac, one of the chief scoffers at Altamira, had publicly admitted his change of heart in an article called *Mea Culpa d'un Sceptique*. Stone Age Art was an accepted fact.

Amongst the first-comers who copied the engravings of La Mouthe was an enthusiastic and energetic young cleric named Henri Breuil. Besides taking part in the discovery of the neighbouring caves, he had impressed Cartailhac with the standard of his copying work. The latter, now repentant of his previous scorn at the reports of Altamira, took the young Breuil there. The result was a fanatical and excited study of the famous paintings. The technique of covering the paintings and engravings with tracing paper and copying them that way, which had done well enough in the French caves, would not work here. For one thing many of the bison, horses, deer, and boar were painted on the roof of the cave, and for another the red, orange, and black paint was liable to come off on the other side of the paper. Instead, Breuil lay on his back on sacks of fern in the damp cold and in three weeks, with the help of a long geometrical measuring pole, copied the drawings as exactly as he could.

The same intense enthusiasm and concentration was still there nearly fifty years later when, in South Africa, the Abbé, as he now was, first saw the famous 'White Lady' of Brandberg. Some archaeologists think this drawing represents a Bantu fertility rite of perhaps the eighteenth century.

The Abbé believes it may show the penetration of a Mediterranean white race to South Africa probably two or three thousand years ago. In any case he refused to leave the rock shelter where it was found for a moment during the ten days after he first saw it, and slept and ate there while he studied it (Pl. 12).

In the meantime his industrious copying, deciphering, and studying of Stone Age art had spread knowledge of it far and wide.

The subject is so visual that it fairly cried out for a Buried Treasure programme on it, and the occasion Dr Daniel and I had long awaited came with an Arts Council exhibition of the Abbé's drawings and a visit by the Abbé himself. He was not anxious to subject an audience to his English, but happily agreed to be filmed showing how he had made the drawings, when the famous enthusiasm at once made itself apparent. No sooner had I told him what we wanted him to do next than he had started. No waiting for lights, cameras, or cues, only a slight puzzlement that we couldn't quite keep up all the time with his great pace.

The last thing I asked him to do was to trace the famous white lady of Brandberg, as he had done when he first saw her. Here the shoe was on the other foot. Once he started he was so carried away by his enthusiasm that nothing would stop him until he had finished it. Lights, camera, crew had all packed up and gone but there he was at the end of a long and tiring day, still tracing away indefatigably. I did not complain because not many people have a copy of the white lady signed by the Abbé Breuil.

We began the actual programme with the question of the date of the art. The Abbé does not agree with all archaeologists about this.

Through study of the development of tricks of style and by carefully unravelling the way some of the paintings and engravings overlay each other, the Abbé has worked out a chronology, divided into six periods. In some cases these periods can be related to tools of certain types, bones of extinct animals, and the comings and goings of the Ice Ages, which left their traces in the first 50,000 years B.C. The earliest examples the Abbé considers date back to about 40,000 B.C. However, atomic physics has recently produced another way of estimating their age. A carbon 14 dating for some charcoal found in a cave with drawings of one of the Abbé's earlier periods gave a much later date, about 12,000 B.C. Carbon 14 dating, roughly speaking, is done by measuring the amount of radio activity given off by the carbon contained in an object. This decreases at a given rate, and therefore indicates the age, but as there is a lack of suitable material, and it might not, in any case, be contemporary with the painting, there is no means as yet of finally settling the question. All that is agreed is that the art must be at least 10,000 years old, if not older.

This much of the story was described by Dr Daniel in his own characteristic way actually at the exhibition of the Abbé's drawings, as the cameras moved round illustrating his points with the relevant pictures. But television really came into its own when we started to show how the paintings were done. For this we were able to get Mr Miles Burkitt, a former pupil of the Abbé Breuil and a lecturer in Archaeology at Cambridge since 1921, to give a most convincing and informative demonstration of the possible methods. Several pieces of stone, he explained, have been found with marks of burning on one end, as well as a more elaborate, thick, triangular piece hollowed out on the top. This primitive lamp, like those of the Eskimos, was probably filled with animal fat, with a wick of twisted moss. Skulls may also have been used for the same purpose. Flame to light the lamps might have been got by rubbing a stick rapidly over an old hollow log filled with dried leaves and straw, as the Australian aborigines do to-day, or by striking sparks off flint, but their method, whatever it was, must have been a handy one, because such feeble lamps would have been easily put out by the dampness and draughts of the caves.

The colours used were generally red, black, and yellow. Natural ochres produced the reds and yellows. Black came from manganese dioxide and charcoal. All these would be ground to powder between pieces of sandstone, and mixed with melted fat before being put on the walls. They may have also used vegetable material, like berries, or even blood, but no traces of this would survive.

Paint-brushes made from animal hairs stuck in small bones or pads of moss would be obvious means for applying the paint. More remarkable were the stamps or seals used to produce the series of dots which are used in some of the caves to represent the animals in an almost impressionistic manner. These were probably pieces of wood with flat ends round which pieces of skin were tied. They were dabbed in the liquid paint and then pressed on to the surface of the rock. All these were demonstrated in the programme with the actual materials by Mr Burkitt.

Another possible tool is the blowpipe. Some of the animals at Lascaux are painted with a cloudy texture that thins away at the edges. This may have been done by blowing powdered paint either off the palm of the hand or through a hollow bone on to a surface specially smeared with fat on which the paint would stick. Some archaeologists, however, think this is too far-fetched an idea and that the hollow bones with remains of paint in them were merely the artist's paint-holders.

What is certain is that much care and preparation went into the work. Probably the artist first outlined his subject by scratching it on the rock with a sharp flint. Many of these engraving tools survive. Then he would sketch with paint over the engraved outline and finally shade in the whole animal. You can see this very clearly in the Lascaux rhinoceros, part of whose belly has been sketched in but not completed like the rest of the animal.

Engraving itself reached a very high standard. In some of the caves no painting survives, but amongst the maze of overlapping lines cut in the stone there are some very skilful impressions of animals engraved with the most extraordinary simplicity and strength.

But this skill was not achieved at once. Mr Burkitt thinks that man's earliest efforts are probably the wavy lines which he found he could make by drawing his fingers smeared with paint over the walls of the caves, in imitation of the clawmarks of the bears who previously had inhabited them. Gorillas have been known to trace the outline of their shadow with a finger. Stone Age Man certainly traced the outline of his hands, presumably by holding one against the stone and blowing soot or paint round it from the palm of the other, leaving the outline of the hand.

These negative hands, as they are called, have two other interesting points about them. They show that their owners were largely right-handed, and may also have had a practice that anthropologists have reported still exists in New Guinea today. There amongst some of the primitive tribes it is a custom to cut off a finger, as a token of mourning, rage, or vengeance.

From these early efforts, the artists went on to paint and engrave animals with increasing skill. The animals are nearly always shown in profile, but not usually photographically, because some parts, like the horns and hoofs, are shown full face. This is known as twisted perspective, an awkward phrase but easy enough to understand once you see an animal painted this way.

The animals are nearly always shown singly or in pairs facing each other, or following each other in single file. There is no background scenery, or trees or plants, and human beings, on the rare occasions when they are shown, are done in a curious cartoon style, like schoolboy caricatures, that look very odd beside the animals which are drawn with such brilliant accuracy and skill. There are one or two strange-shaped objects that have been interpreted as round skin tents or reed houses, and at Lascaux particularly there are several geometrically shaped objects known as 'blazons', a not very helpful word which is taken from heraldry. They may have been symbolic signs or, more likely perhaps, traps. It is thought that Stone Age hunters used to try to drive herds of game over cliffs, from the piles of bones that have been found at the bottom of some, and so they might well also have used square pit-traps, as the pygmies of Africa do today.

But these are all incidentals. The main subject is always animals—bison, mammoth, ox, horse, bear, and reindeer, which we know from the deposits of bones were all hunted by Stone Age Man.

It is generally believed that this gives a clue to the purpose of this art. On these animals depended the artists' very existence. When the game was plentiful and easily caught, then there would be leisure time to do these paintings, but of course they were done for a purpose. They were not there just to decorate the caves where people lived. The paintings are often deep in the caves, in very inaccessible places, where it would be most uncomfortable and inconvenient, as well as cold, to settle. Nor are the caves decorated tombs, such as occur later in history. They have produced no signs of ceremonial burial. As Dr Daniel said in our programme they are temples, where the paintings were done in ceremonies to gain power over the animals to be hunted. By drawing an animal, you gain power over it. This is the ancient principle of sympathetic magic, common all over the world, and still surviving to recent times in some places in the habit of making wax models of your enemies and sticking pins in them.

The Australian aborigines are a people still living a Stone Age life today, and for the programme I managed to obtain some film which illustrated this parallel most vividly. They wander from place to place, living by hunting, carrying all their possessions with them, with no settled homes and making their tools out of stone, bone, and wood. They hold ceremonies, just as Stone Age Man must have done, to gain power and success over their prey, only in this case it is the kangaroo that is the object. Elaborate drawings are made in the sand, and in dances the man representing the kangaroo ends by pretending to fall dead, successfully hunted by his companions, so that by representing what they want to happen they try to ensure that it will.

The Stone Age animals painted in the caves are those that would be hunted for food. Many are shown with arrows or spears sticking in them. Numerous others are heavy with young. Many, too, are drawn on top of each other, as if it was the actual act of painting not the final result that mattered.

Recognizable scenes are very rare, but the most famous, the wounded bison at Lascaux, is a hunting one. In this group a disembowelled and dying bison, pierced by a spear, stands beside a cartoon man, falling or lying on the ground, drawn with a bird's head and only four fingers on each hand. A number of people think he had had his neck dislocated by the bison first. Anyway, a little further away is the spear thrower, which must have launched the spear that struck the bison, and a stick with a bird's head on it also. Finally, a rhinoceros is walking away from the scene (Pl. 8).

What does it mean? Was some hunter decoying the bison by pretending to be a couple of birds in the undergrowth, while his companions crept up on the bison from behind, in the same way as the Aborigines hunt kangaroo today, when the decoy-man was killed by a rhinoceros that appeared unexpectedly? One cannot tell, but it is intriguing to imagine why it was painted.

I wondered if it was such an extraordinary incident that some artist felt he had to record it. Perhaps it was some great chief who was the victim, or perhaps the artist hoped to revenge himself on the rhinoceros for killing a friend. Once can only guess, but the scene points the parallels with the Aborigines, who use decoys in this way, and it does underline the significance of hunting in the art.

There remains the final question. Were the creators of these paintings consciously artists? Were they aware of composition and beauty? Looking at some of the Lascaux drawings, I think most people would find hard to believe that the painter did not have some artistic feeling for his subject, whatever the magical impulses involved. Some, surely, are the work of an artist as well as a priest and magician, who gloried in the shape of his work as well as in its purpose.

But artist, priest, and hunter alike were dependent on their surroundings. When the climate changed, their art died. Ice-sheets shrank, forests appeared, and the great herds of game that had supported the old Stone Age peoples vanished.

Man, the archaeologists tell you, was by now sufficiently adaptable to remain, though his way of life had to change. This is known technically as the transition from the Palaeolithic, or Old Stone Age, to the Mesolithic or Middle Stone Age. From a hunter on the wild, open uplands, man became a scavenger on the fringe of the forest and sea-shore. His diet changed from mammoth flesh and wild horses to shellfish and hazel nuts. His flint tools changed to those suitable for clearing the fringe of the forest or hunting small game and birds. The bone harpoon that some fisherman dropped from his dug-out canoe in the marshy shallows of the North Sea, for it to be dredged up in another fisherman's net thousands of years later, and the antler head-dress some priest or hunter wore at Star Carr in Yorkshire, illuminate this period. We have not yet done a Buried Treasure programme on one of the Mesolithic sites. I hope to remedy this one day, but though interesting, this period seemed to me to lack the spectacular visual remains of the climax of Stone Age art and the next great step forward.

1. The Piltdown Site. From right to left: Dawson, Smith Woodward, Veness Hargreaves, their chief helper, working on the site beside the drive of Barlsham Manor from which came most of the Piltdown finds. Chipper, the goose, usually came to the site when Dawson was at work.

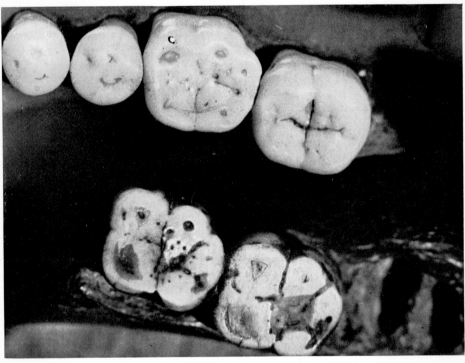

2 & 3. ABOVE. A side view of the Piltdown jaw. BELOW. The unnaturally flat wear of the two Piltdown molars (below) compared to the more normal dimpled wear of a set of human molars.

4 & 5. ABOVE. Dr Kenneth Oakley testing one of the Piltdown eoliths for staining at the British Museum (Natural History). BELOW. One of the great Acheulian hand axes.

6 & 7. ABOVE. The frieze of stags' heads at Lascaux. BELOW. The paintings on the walls of the main chamber at Lascaux. The great oxen are more than life size.

8 & 9. ABOVE. The dying bison at Lascaux. The hunter's spear lies across the disembowelled bison and the spear-thrower is by the hunter's feet. BELOW. Part of the paintings on the wall of the main chamber at Lascaux.

10 & 11. ABOVE. The painted roof of one of the passages at Lascaux. Above the horse is one of the mysterious signs that may represent traps. BELOW. The Abbé Breuil in front of one of his drawings of Stone Age art. Note the spears embedded in the bison's side.

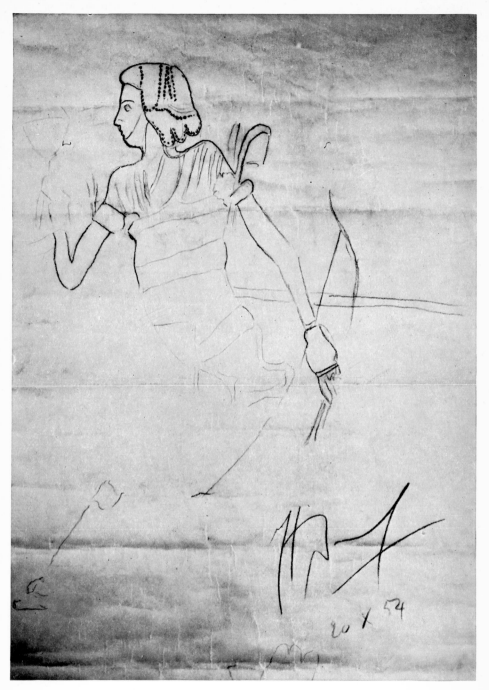

12. A drawing of the White Lady of Brandberg by the Abbé Breuil which he presented to the author.

13 & 14. ABOVE. The mound or tell which hides the remains of the ancient cities of Jericho. In the foreground are some of the mud-houses of the refugee village. Behind the tell is the oasis of Jericho and the modern town. The Dead Sea is at the foot of the distant mountains. BELOW. The headquarters of the Jericho excavation camp, taken from the tell which conceals the ruins of the ancient cities of Jericho. In the foreground white-clad women from the refugee village are filling water jars at Elisha's spring. Behind the headquarters house is part of the oasis of Jericho, and in the distance across the valley of the Jordan are the mountains of Gilead.

15 & 16. ABOVE. Two of the basket boys at Jericho. The hat of the one on the right is made from a fox fur. It was probably rather hot, but easily the outstanding headgear on the excavation. BELOW. Lady Wheeler in the burial chamber of a Bronze Age grave near Jericho. Besides the remains of fourteen bodies, wooden furnishings, mats, remains of food, and even flesh were preserved probably by the fumes in the Dead Valley soil which kill bacteria.

17. The great 50-foot deep main trench of the excavations at Jericho. The lowest of the walls revealed by the trench is the earliest town wall known to us. Beneath it is the defensive ditch hewn into bedrock, evidence of efficient community organization possibly as early as 7000 B.C.

18. Filming the opening of a Bronze Age grave at Jericho.

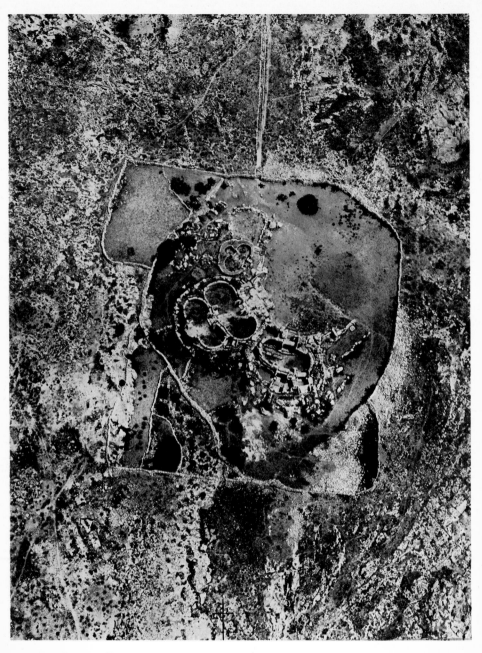

19. Aerial view of the prehistoric Maltese temples of M'Naidra. The smallest one, at the top, is of the earliest clover-leaf plan type. In the later centre one, the plan has become two adjacent ovals.

20 & 21. ABOVE. Filming the megalithic temple of M'Naidra from a lorry borrowed from the Electricity Company. BELOW. The main chamber of the Gigantija temple in Gozo. The figure in the foreground gives a measure of the size.

22 & 23. ABOVE. The main altar in the Temple of Hal Tarxien in Malta. Compare the skill and accuracy of the stonework with the roughness of the Gigantija. BELOW. Filming a frieze of sacrificial animals in the Temple of Hal Tarxien in Malta.

24 & 25. ABOVE. John Evans holding a sacrificial flint knife which was found in the hole in the altar where the last priest to use it had left it 3,500 years ago. BELOW. The main chamber of the Hypogeum of Hal Saflieni in Malta. More than 7,000 bodies were buried in this extraordinary underground catacomb. The rock has been carved in imitation of the megalithic style of the temples above ground.

26 & 27. ABOVE. John Evans standing beside the remains of a great stone figure of a neolithic Maltese goddess of fertility. The upper part and feet are missing. BELOW. A small terracotta model of a sleeping prophetess from a neolithic temple in Malta.

CHAPTER IV

THE WALLS OF JERICHO

————

No one knows how man began to speak. Even the most primitive known modern people, the Tasmanian aborigines, had a complicated grammar and large vocabulary. It is a far cry from that to the varying emotions expressed by the chattering of monkeys, or the different notes by which a cock calls attention to an enemy or a mouthful of food. How the gap was bridged we can only guess.

Both gestures and onomatopoeia, that is, calling a dog a bow-wow in imitation of the sound he makes, have been ruled out, because neither explain how man became able to express thought, or ideas, by a sound. You can express a situation like hunger or danger by a gesture, but not an idea or an object. Language developed, how or when remains a mystery, to control behaviour, and pass on ideas and concepts.

The first use of fire has been imagined often enough by writers from Lucretius onwards, the timely flash of lighting, the tamed forest fire, the cast-aside chunk of meat rescued from the ashes, but again no one knows for certain when this happened. All that can be said is that one moment there is no trace of it and the next there is. Pekin man used fire. Whether he could make it is uncertain. Only the Andamanese, of modern primitive people, cannot light it in any way and so perpetually treasure a naturally kindled flame.

What is known is how and when man became a settled being. From being a wanderer, living by catching or collecting what he could, dependent on the fluctuating bounty of nature, he became a farmer and a stock-breeder. This was the most significant moment in man's history. It made civilization possible. In technical terms this is the change from the Palaeolithic, or Old Stone Age, and Mesolithic, or Middle Stone Age, to the Neolithic, or New Stone Age. From being a savage, man is promoted to being a barbarian.

In the savage, food-gathering stage, man hardly differed from a pack of wolves in the skill on which his life depended, and he was as much a parasite on nature as a fungus on an ivy plant. Only control of fire, which

c

gave him a wider choice of food, and tools, which increased his adapta-
bility, reduced very slightly his utter dependence on what nature provided
ready to eat.

It was normal in these circumstances to face the constant threat of
starvation. All who could had to hunt or collect food. All that was found
was eaten. No one could live mainly by making tools, because there was no
guarantee that the others would find enough food above their own needs
to barter for the specialist's handiwork.

There were, of course, times when this was not so. The buffalo hunters
of America, before Columbus' arrival, could put aside a surplus of pem-
mican for lean months or barter. The Eskimos did the same with dried
fish. The cave art of the Old Stone Age was made possible by a local
abundance of game. The mammoth-hunters of the Ukraine probably
had the same good fortune at the same time.

But it was the Neolithic revolution that made feasible a reasonably
dependable surplus of food, and its resulting possibilities. It has been
calculated that nine city families can be fed by one Middle Western
American farming family. Neolithic man obviously did not do as well as
that. Often, if he was unsuccessful at hunting too, he must have gone very
hungry by the tenth or eleventh month after harvest. But at least he could
now remain in one place, share ideas between larger groups, and support a
few specialists.

The first signs of this vital change are therefore particularly fascinating.

One is found amongst the Natufians, the cave-dwellers of Mount Carmel
in Palestine. It is a grooved bone sickle, set with flint teeth which have
the peculiar gloss that comes from constant brushing against plant stalks.
This is one of the earliest known agricultural implements, and was used
about 5,500 B.C. to cut wild barley and emmer, a rough form of wheat.
Whether some intelligent Natufian woman realized what would happen
if a handful of seeds from these were dropped in the ground is not known,
but obviously it was only a step to agriculture proper.

For one of the earliest agricultural settlements, where we know this
actually happened, you must go to Jarmo, east of the Tigris in the foot-
hills of north-eastern Iraq. Here, peasant farmers living in simple clay
houses with floors of reeds cultivated the most primitive type of wheat
and barley at a date given by a carbon 14 test as between 5,270 and 4,630
B.C. They used sickles and weighted digging sticks in the fields and saddle
querns, hollow stones with a movable top, to grind the grain. Their
women, no longer limited to possessions which they could carry on them,
made equally important changes inside the home.

Clay-lined pits in their floors which had been hardened by fire give a clue to the possible origin of the pottery that appears later, and impressions in mud tell of the use of the earliest known plain-weave mats. In the Egyptian sites of Fayum and Badari, only a little later than Jarmo, these mats are accompanied by linen, the earliest known example of weaving. I have put in this rough summary of what I had learnt from reading the works of Dr Oakley, Dr Carleton Coon, Professor Gordon Childe, and others because it explains why I was so excited when I heard that all these sites had been surpassed by some excavations which seemed to show that the neolithic revolution, the start of civilization, had in fact happened some two thousand years earlier than the previously accepted date. Here was a most important opportunity for 'Buried Treasure'.

The trouble was that these excavations were a long and expensive journey away for a camera team. They had been going on every season since 1951 at Jericho in the Hashemite kingdom of Jordan. However, the Director of the excavations, Dr Kathleen Kenyon, was very willing to co-operate in a programme, Sir Mortimer Wheeler declared they were the most important excavations anywhere since the war, which coming from the President of the Society of Antiquaries was no light judgment, and 'Buried Treasure' had now been running for two years with apparently unaltered popularity. I therefore decided to suggest Jericho as a programme subject. The BBC authorities approved and in February 1956 I found myself in the Middle East for the first time, in a state of considerable excitement as Damascus, Jordan, Abana and Pharphar and Jerusalem changed before one's eyes from legend to reality.

We landed at Jerusalem airport, met Dr Kenyon and Lady Wheeler, who was one of her assistants, and drove past the scarlet anemones that sprinkled the rocky hill-sides, the wild lupins and olive trees, down fifteen hairpin bends skilfully engineered by the Arab Legion in one half mile, to the valley of the Jordan. The mound that covers the remains of the twenty-two ancient cities of Jericho is less impressive than its surroundings. To the west, the Mount of Temptation, a smooth, barren brown, towers over the tell. To the north lies the refugee village where 20,000 refugees from the part of Palestine which is now Israel are housed in little flat-roofed mud huts. To the east the clouds chase soft purple, green, and grey patches across the valley of the Jordan. To the south, a leaden rim of the Dead Sea lies between the oasis which contains modern Jericho and the distant mountains (Pl. 13).

But the brown, untidy tell, as they call these mounds made up of the layered remains of ancient towns, contains a remarkable core. At the bottom of a 50-foot trench, impressive in itself, stands a rough stone wall with a circular tower set into it, guarded by a 30-foot wide ditch cut into the bedrock (Pl. 17). This belongs to the earliest known town in history. Piled above are many, many layers that yielded no pottery, and so apparently belong to that mouthful of a period, 'the pre-pottery neolithic'. At Jarmo, there are far fewer comparable layers. It does not necessarily follow that Jericho is that much earlier, but a carbon 14 dating seems to confirm that the rough stone wall, the tower with its amazing stairway inside, and the ditch that alone must have been a mighty labour, move the known beginnings of civilization back possibly two thousand years.

There were many other exciting things at Jericho, the early Bronze Age walls of mud bricks made by the same methods as those we filmed in use in the refugee village, the great Middle Bronze Age wall and smooth-plastered slope that further hampered its attackers, and the Bronze Age tombs whose contents were so well preserved that from the bodies lying amongst the profuse furnishings of still-surviving wood, mats, and food, the excavators were able to collect actual flesh, 3,500 years old, which I brought back for them to London for analysis and study of the blood groups at Westminster hospital (Pl. 16).

We had other excitements too. Our filming visit coincided with the dismissal of Glubb Pasha. The day after this happened, the Palestinian refugees, who had been celebrating as though it were a great victory, started to break up the party which the excavators were giving the work-men on the dig. Their excuse was our filming of an Arabic charade in which there were some men dressed as women. We stopped the filming, but for an unpleasant quarter of an hour one began to get the feel of what mob violence might be like, as a band of two hundred or so stood in an undecided group just beyond the range of the lights on the house, occasionally hurling a stone in the direction of the excavation headquarters. Then they went home and left Dr Kenyon and her helpers to their pre-pottery neolithic and us to our filming.

This involved two problems and a disappointment. The disappointment was that hardly anything survived that could definitely be called Joshua's Jericho. Though the mound was still over 70 feet high, nearly all the buildings of the later occupations had collapsed and been washed away, as the rain dissolved their mud bricks. The two difficulties were that the sharp contrast between the heavy shadows of the deep trenches and the bright sunlight made filming difficult, and none of the excavations, apart from the tombs, were very exciting to look at.

However, an answer was all around, particularly in our ears. The life of the dig seemed to me much more Victorian than modern in its epic character. The constant strangeness of the sounds, the Arabic chatter, the singing of the basket boys, the monkey and camel cries, underlined to me Dr Kenyon's achievement in running this enterprise.

The dig itself was large in physical size. After the sparse pickings of an English excavation, the finds were enormously prolific. Its impact on archaeology was likely to be far-reaching. English, Canadians, Americans, Danes, Dutch, and Germans were involved. There were four hundred Arab workmen to recruit, train, and handle. The local situation had all sorts of complexities. The organization of food, accommodation, materials, and storage alone was a feat. And all this was run, and very happily too, by a woman.

It seemed, therefore, quite legitimate to me to concentrate as much on the circumstances of the dig as on the results. We filmed Fatmeh doing the washing and the vast grey tea-pot in the middle of the breakfast table as well as the plastered skulls, the astonishing portrait pieces of clay modelled into features, with shells as eyes, over actual skulls which the ancient Jerichoans buried under their houses. We recorded on tape Lady Wheeler playing an Arab drum after dinner, as well as the singing of the workmen as they cleared the burnished plaster floors with the rounded corners with which the late Stone Age inhabitants of the tell made housekeeping easier. The pay parade, as the pick and shovel men and the basket boys advanced one by one out of the darkness by Elisha's spring to add their thumb marks or signatures to the list on the brightly lit desk where the director and assistant sat, seemed to me almost as dramatic a subject for the camera as looking down a 15-foot shaft in the refugee village when the round stone at the bottom was hauled away to reveal yet another Bronze Age burial.

But amongst all this harsh but rich mixture of events which we were trying to translate onto film, I found myself constantly going back to that town wall, tower, and ditch at the bottom of the big trench. To see and know about this new evidence of the start of civilization before the rest of the world was very much an experience to hoard and enjoy.

Sir Mortimer Wheeler, who was with us part of the time, told me he thinks the domestication of animals may also have started at somewhere like Jericho. Animals, like humans, would have been attracted to an oasis, thus providing opportunities for their capture. The same conditions applied before that to the scavenging wild dogs who were attracted to the camps of Stone Age man and so became the first domesticated beasts. Reindeer, too, were apparently first tamed through their eagerness for salty matter, particularly human urine. This craving comes from the lack of salt in melted snow, the only available water, and attracted them to human camps, where it was fairly easy to catch the young ones. Like sheep and goats, reindeer could wander with their nomadic owners.

To sum up what I learnt from Dr Kenyon and Sir Mortimer, the Neo-lithic revolution saw in about 7,000 B.C. the start of agriculture and the breeding of domestic animals. This occurred in the 'fertile crescent' stretching between Persia and Egypt. The resulting food surplus, in-creased population, and greater chances of social life and interchange of ideas in a settled state led to much progress. Pottery, spinning, weaving, and the polishing of stone tools were practised by part-time specialists. The progress of man had made a most significant step. By altering the face of the earth and developing special characteristics in animals and plants he had begun to alter the forces of nature.

The next great advance after that was brought about by intensification of what already went on rather than by any revolutionary change, such as from hunting to farming. Gordon Childe has called it 'the Urban Re-volution', the change from barbarism to civilization. This was based on a more intensive use of farming land. The plough, by harnessing animal power, increased the area one man could cultivate. That man could now support more people, including full-time specialists. These would live in groups because it was easier then to distribute their handiwork and store the food which the scattered farms sent in to support them. In this way formerly self-sufficient villages became cities, like Jericho, of people who lived not by what they grew or bred but by barter for their services or skills. Once it became possible to live in a non self-sufficient group it was as easy to barter for luxuries as for essentials, so trade increased.

The discovery of metal accentuated this. Copper and tin were not found near any of the great cities, and their finding, transport, and working involved long distances and careful organization.

It also involved a new development, war. As barbarism turned into civilization, war became a practical proposition, and Jericho had to have its walls. The first farmers, scraping a living from the soil with their primitive hoes, had no time for it. Cities made it possible. The pressure of expanding populations on the available land and trade rivalries pro-vided one cause. The tempting richness, to poorer peoples outside, of the cities was another. Copper changed from a luxury to a necessity very quickly because it made so much more effective weapons than stone. Battle-axes are found more and more frequently as the Stone Age turns into the Bronze Age.

All this needed a quite different sort of organization from that of a farming village. Some records, for instance, had to be made of the goods brought in from the surrounding farms, so writing developed. The earliest known example is on some clay tablets from the temple of Inana at Erech, on which the Sumerian priests about 3,500 B.C. had scratched signs, thought to be numbers, opposite pictures of objects like animals, fishes, plants, and so on. Calendars, and astronomy and mathematics on which to base them, would obviously be essential too, and they developed in the same way. At Jericho, a stone was found carved with a doodle which some people thought might be an illustration of Pythagoras' theorem. Mathematics would be necessary for the planning of community projects like irrigation canals and granaries, which provided food for city populations. Babylonian schoolboys had to solve problems about the area that could be flooded by the water in a cistern of given size, and there were formulas to calculate the work-quotas of the men digging the irrigation canals and the amount of barley needed to feed them. The experts who practised these new skills were the kings and priests. Thereby they added to their prestige as intermediaries with the incalculable deities, who regulated the weather, the harvest, good health, and the other imponderables of man's life. The more complicated life grew, the more urgent it was to have the unseen forces on one's side.

This change from village farming to a literate city existence was thought to have first occurred shortly after 3,500 B.C. in Mesopotamia, and then in the Nile and Indus valleys. The evidence at Jericho may now move this date back three thousand years, though there is no evidence that the culminating invention of writing occurred then. The same process also happened much later in the New World, in central America, and in Peru. These areas were all in nearly tropical lands where intensive farming could produce enough food from a small area to support quite a large population. The Tigris and Euphrates, Nile and Indus, also enabled large quantities of bulky foodstuffs to be moved a considerable way to the various cities. From there expanding populations, the search for metals, and the need for new farming land gradually spread wheels, sails, money, measures, and the other ideas and influences of civilization across the world.

CHAPTER V

THE MALTESE MEGALITHS

LONG BEFORE ARCHAEOLOGY became a subject for television programmes, the BBC successfully broadcast many archaeological sound talks
and features. But this is a field where I think television has a great advantage over sound radio. So much archaeology depends on the evidence of
material remains. Many words may fail to convey what a picture can do
in an instant.

With history, the boot is on the other foot. Ideas and written evidence
are difficult television material. On sound, they are no problem. But one
'Buried Treasure' subject I did borrow straight from the Third Programme, the great prehistoric temples of Malta.

I had always found the early evidences of religion interesting. No
animal knows he must die, but somewhere along the line of evolution,
man's developing imagination harnessed him with the penalty of this
knowledge. His efforts since that moment, to understand and deal with
the incomprehensible powers which govern his fate, have produced
religion.

In the various authorities, you can read about the earliest known
manifestations. The awareness of death was countered by a belief in an
after life. The spirits of the dead, which this idea created, then had to be
considered.

I learned that the fisherman amongst the primitive Stone Age peoples
of today who have been studied by anthropologists threw his first catch
of the season back into the lake, however hungry he was, because it
might placate these spirits. Eating the heart or brain of your victim or
enemy might add his strength to yours in facing them. Special pre-
cautions might stop them adding their share of troubles to the ever
present dangers and difficulties of life.

Neanderthal man took the trouble to bury his dead. The Stone Age
hunters and artists went further and covered some of their dead with
red ochre, like the 'red lady' of Paviland, who in fact was a young man
ceremonially buried in South Wales with his personal ornaments, an ele-

phant's head, and a covering of ochre. Whether this was to give the dead vitality in the after-life or just a ceremonial treatment is not relevant. It shows that already man was concerned with the idea of death.

In the museum of Les Eyzies, near Lascaux, you can see a reconstruction of a burial of Old Stone Age date which had an odd little structure of stones on top of it.

Once people settled in one place, the possibilities of this type of activity became far greater. No band of hunters could raise a large monument, even if they wanted to, because they could not support large numbers in one place for long. Agriculture and a settled life changed that. The next stage of man's history is marked by the great communal monuments which appeasement of the gods, concern with the after-life, or pleas for fertility drove him to build.

In Egypt, the Pharaohs' burial place developed from a hole in the desert to the Pyramids. In Mesopotamia, Ziggurats were erected, great stepped mounds on which stood temples. But even in places far from such centres of imminent civilization, monuments of various types appear in this period. As the next great expression of early man that is visible to us today, after Stone Age art, they are the subject of much curiosity. Generally they are called Megaliths. This comes from the Greek words *megas*—great, and *lithos*—stone. From the latter root come also the names which archaeologists have given to the three great divisions of the Stone Age:

Palaeolithic period —old Stone Age — 1,000,000 — 10,000 B.C.
Mesolithic period —middle Stone Age — 10,000 — 5,000 B.C.
Neolithic period —new Stone Age — 7,000 — 3,000 B.C.

These dates are only rough approximations, which vary in different places. The Neolithic revolution, for instance, which started between 7000 and 5000 B.C. in the Middle East, did not reach Britain until probably 2500 B.C. or even later.

One of the best places to see the development of a Neolithic community's megaliths is Malta. This could not have been said before 1953. While the great stone temples and the burial places of Malta have long impressed and interested inhabitants and visitors alike, they have been a puzzle to historians. The dry, sunny air and the amount of easily available stone have helped to preserve them. In their great size and complicated patterns, they have been described as the work of different peoples who were supposed to have been the source of all Mediterranean civilizations and the Phoenicians, who flourished from 800-200 B.C.

Now, thanks largely to the work of Professor John Evans, we can
understand them far more clearly. Professor Evans, then a Cambridge
graduate in archaeology, was put in charge of the field-work when a
commision was set up by the Royal Malta University, helped by a grant
from the Colonial Office through the Inter-Universities Council, to study
the temples.

It was a broadcast about the work of the Commission which introduced
me to the subject. As I have explained, I thought the whole subject of the
early manifestations of religion was very interesting to the layman, and
the Maltese part of it seemed particularly suited to Television. The
temples were picturesque, all the evidence was easily accessible, they
belonged to a very interesting stage of man's religious development, and
their dating made a good coherent story. Thus it was that I found myself
one March morning setting off with Professor Evans to have it all explained to me and to see if the reality in Malta matched my expectations.

By narrow unsignposted roads, past futuristic prickly pears and the
neatly knit fields with their tiers of stone walls stretching away on each
side except where pitted rock prevented cultivation, we drove to M'Garr.
This is a village in the south-west of the island with the usual collection
of white, brown, and yellow flat-topped houses, like a child's toy town,
clustered round the huge dome raised by the devout Maltese, which
makes almost every church on the island look like a cathedral. Down a
side street, in the fringe between field and back-yard, there were what
appeared to be a series of sheep-pens of low walls made from small
rough stones, the ruins of the temple. Across the front of the pens ran
the most impressive part, a façade of large stone blocks with a dumpy
entrance in the middle. Unhesitatingly John Evans pointed out the
oldest part with its clover-leaf shape for, like almost all these temples,
it was constantly added to and built over. Certainly anyone could see it
was crudely built and simple in shape, but it was hard at first to understand the basis of his certainty.

It was only gradually that I came to appreciate the vast amount of
patient combing of material and information that lay behind it.

Professor Evans's first task had been to sort out the great mass of
pottery that was found in the various sites. From this he got a sequence
of styles which he was able to date by reference to similar Sicilian and
Greek styles of known date. The next step was to test this sequence by
excavation. Professor Stuart Piggott, Professor of Prehistoric Archaeology at Edinburgh who, with Mr J. B. Ward-Perkins, Director of the
British School at Rome, advised the Commission, described in a broadcast
their feelings as the trial trenches went down through the successive

floor levels of the temples, and a mass of pieces of pottery appeared below each in exactly the right order. 'We got quite hilarious about it,' he said 'and it wasn't just the sunny salty air and Xaghra wine, though they certainly helped. It was the recognition that our theoretical archaeological methods, when put to the test of practical excavation, did in fact justify themselves.'

I have tried the Xaghra wine and I should have ascribed any hilarity to the successful archaeological methods. It is the colour of varnish, costs 4d a bottle, which is usually a lemonade bottle, and is not to be missed, but a bottle at lunch-time induces sleep rather than cheerful digging.

The temple next in date after M'Garr is just beside the village of Xaghra, which is on the island of Gozo. To go there we had to get up before breakfast and drive from Valletta past the bay where St Paul is said to have been shipwrecked, to the little harbour at the western end of the island. There we drove the car over heaving, creaking planks onto the ferry, which was already rocking considerably even alongside. Rikki, the assistant cameraman, looked decidedly thoughtful. The ferry was small, we had had no breakfast, and the strait between the islands is a notoriously lively piece of water. However, breakfast at the 'Duke of Edinburgh', Gozo's chief pub, made up for everything. We had bacon and eggs under the banana tree on the terrace, with a lemon orchard stretching away in the sun in front of us. England's March dreariness, which we had been enduring a few days before, seemed marvellously remote.

Gozo is wilder and less crowded than Malta. The ground swoops up into conical hills, on one of which the citadel of Rabat makes a fairy-tale skyline with its walls and towers.

The Gigantija, the tower of the giants, is in keeping. It is easily the most impressive of the Neolithic temples of the islands. It stands on the brow of a hill, and its back wall of great pock-marked, unworked stones towers up some 40 feet. An uncemented wall of great boulders that high is a very striking sight. Some of the huge stones at the base are 18 feet long and weigh about 50 tons. A man standing in the main chamber is completely dwarfed (Pl. 21). The simple clover-leaf pattern already has another oval chamber added to it, and the dummy façade at M'Garr has here become a great cliff.

A small stone model from the period, though broken, gives us an idea of what these temples must have looked like originally. They were high, with slightly curved façades about 50 feet high and 90 feet across, carried on at each end by single standing stones. The later ones with their smooth worked stones must have had a curiously twentieth-century look. No one could possibly expect any modern construction to resemble Stonehenge or a pyramid, unless they were deliberate copies, but these neat, tall temples with their flat roofs and blank faces in their original state would not look at all out of place in a contemporary power station.

Professor Evans thought the date of the early part of the Gigantija was probably about 1850 B.C., as opposed to 2100 B.C. for the early part of M'Garr, but he showed us some pieces of stones, probably introduced later, with carvings on them. One had a snake on it and the other a faint row of spirals, which is important. These spirals are very like some in the shaft-graves of Mycenae on the Greek mainland. This Greek influence may have affected the great artistic development in the next stage of the temples.

By the time they were building temples in 1650 B.C., like Hagar Qim or M'Naidra, he explained, they had abandoned the rough slabs of coral-line limestone which they had first used, and taken instead to the softer globigerina limestone, which is easy to shape into blocks and carve. The result is that the temples become far more elaborate and decorated.

Hagar Qim, though it is the only one to which a sign-post directs you and has a pleasant position on a headland looking over the sea, I never liked. It is so complicated in its different stages that it is difficult to sort out. M'Naidra is far more attractive. It is within sight of Hagar Qim but, exceptionally for Malta, it lies in a little rocky valley by the sea that is quite removed from people or houses. Three temples and a fig tree stand in a grassy, walled enclosure just above the cliff. The temples in an aerial photograph show clearly how the clover-leaf shape of the earliest type has turned into two flattened ovals. These are now decorated with all sorts of elaborate niches and altars, and the soft stone is covered with patterns of honeycomb pitting (Pl. 19).

M'Naidra is not as big or as impressive as the Gigantija, but in its peaceful setting by the sea it is a very pleasant place to visit. I say this even though we had anything but a peaceful time there.

After considerable trouble we had hired a lorry with an extensible ladder from the electricity company to get some high angle film shots of the temples. To get it there involved a hair-raising drive along a rock path, not a road, overlooking the sea. The lorry bumped and swayed perilously, but eventually arrived. No sooner had Terry, the cameraman, climbed up the ladder with his gear, than a battery behind the brow of the hill started a practice shoot at a group of rocks out to sea. From the noise and concussion they appeared to be just behind us, and the shells almost to be parting Terry's hair. Half an hour later, having survived the shells, Terry collapsed with food-poisoning. Very soon he was green and practically unconscious. Luckily there was an R.A.F. airfield not far away and we took him to the doctor there. He was all right the next day, but it was a bad moment. Rikki said it was all due to the libation of Xaghra wine we had poured out to the Mother Goddess at our lunch-time picnic in the temple the day before. Terry more prosaically blamed some mussels he had eaten.

The climax of this temple-building was reached about 1450 B.C. at Hal Tarxien. This is in an enclosure, behind a handsome modern Ministry of Works style façade in a side street near Valletta. Passing through a little museum you come to an extraordinary tangle of overlapping walls, chambers, and passages, none of them much over 8 feet in height. It is all rather untidy architecturally and has none of the impressive size of the Gigantija, or the beautiful setting of M'Naidra.

An aerial photograph and further study soon starts to put it in proportion. You can see how the temples overlap, and that in the final form the old clover-leaf shape has become a series of three oval chambers. But the real achievement here is the stonework. Architecturally, some of the great 6-foot blocks have been smoothed so accurately that you can hardly get a knife blade into the joints between them.

Artistically, the richness, assurance, and skill of the sculptured carving of the stone reflect the brilliance achieved at their peak by these Neolithic farmers of Malta. There are carvings of animals—sheep, pig, goats and oxen—spirals, and a decorated scroll-work that would do credit to any designer of any period (Pl. 22).

Then, quite suddenly, this civilization disappears. It does not degenerate, or become modified by another. It simply vanishes. It vanished so abruptly that behind a stone plug in one of the main altars at Hal Tarxien a flint knife used for sacrificing animals was found undisturbed where the last priest to use it had left it some three thousand five hundred years ago (Pl. 24).

Professor Evans thinks it is possible to get some idea of what sort of sudden disaster might have caused this cutting short of a people at the peak of their artistic development. It was probably the invasion of warriors from south-east Italy. They used metal weapons, had pots with strange owls' faces on them, and the reason why they did not take over the temples is clear. Their religion prompted them to burn the dead and bury the ashes with curious idols.

They in turn were invaded by another people from southern Sicily, whose forceful invasion is borne out by the great stone defence wall which the defenders built across the peninsula of Borg-i-Nadur, presumably to protect their beach-head, since it is just by one of the best harbours in the island.

It is not perhaps being too imaginative to get a sense of crude, rough power from this fortification, as compared with the delicate traceries of Hal Tarxien.

My summing up of Professor Evans's theories would be that the history of man in Malta began between 3000 and 2000 B.C. with the colonization of the island by Neolithic farmers from Sicily. These did not build stone temples, but they left traces of their occupation in the great cave of Ghar Dalam, from which have come thousands of bones of pygmy-hippopotami like the one the Piltdown forger stained and planted in Sussex, though of course the hippopotamus bones are from a much earlier period. Professor Evans's excavations and pottery classifications show that by about 2100 B.C., they were building the earliest type of crude stone temple. Its clover-leaf plan gradually developed over the next six hundred years into an elaborate three-chamber type with artistic and highly-skilled stone-work and carving. The simple farming community that had achieved this was then swept away suddenly by an invasion from Sicily of warriors armed with metal weapons. That is probably as definite a picture as archaeology can give.

Their domestic life remains an almost complete blank. We have no idea whether their homes were as well built or decorated as their temples. But there are two problems on which we can throw a little light. Where did the idea of these temples come from, and what went on in them?

Professor Evans thinks he has the answer to the first in certain early tombs cut in the rock. These are kidney-shaped, with an entrance passage. It is not difficult to see how this might have led to the clover-leaf shape of the early temples.

Family tombs cut in the rock are fairly common at this period in the Mediterranean area. One type has a more or less circular plan with a domed roof and a narrow entrance doorway from a forecourt. Some people believe this was originally a copy in rock of the round houses people lived in then, a home during the after-life. In any case, it is easy to see how a copy of the tombs above ground would produce the later temples with forecourt, narrow entrance, and chambers leading off it. Perhaps the ceremonies carried out in front of the tombs became too elaborate or too important to take place in the open, and so temples were built for them.

Professor Evans thinks there may be burial vaults attached to every temple, and that the Hypogeum of Hal Saflieni is typical of the most elaborate type. This Hypogeum is a great underground burial site and is one of the most remarkable places in Malta. You go down a spiral staircase and come to a very complicated collection of chambers, passages, archways, wells and tombs all cut in the rock, which is very soft, at different levels and in different sizes. The Hypogeum extends over an acre and goes down to 40 feet in depth, where in the lowest level the water drips into empty vaults that were abandoned before any bodies were put there. In the other vaults remains of more than 7,000 skeletons have been found, and there are still plenty of others uncounted. The roof of one chamber has spirals painted in red, like the carved spirals in the temples, and some of the rock is carved to resemble the architecture of the temples, a reverse of the process which produced the temples as copies originally of tombs (Pl. 25).

It is an extraordinary place, not particularly eerie, because the roofs are high and the chambers wide, but it would be no joke to be down there if the lights failed. The passages are so complicated, and the floors so slippery with pools of water everywhere, that it would be easy to fall down one of the holes or wells, and add another body to the 7,000.

There are stories of a similar vault near the Gigantija, though nobody knows where, and if the theory is right, there should be one connected with every temple. There are the remains of between thirty and forty temples known, so if you have a way of finding underground chambers in the rock, Malta is the place to go.

Surprisingly, there is quite a lot of material to tell us what went on in the temples, though you must remember, as Professor Piggott has said, that trying to understand their religion from these objects is like trying to discover Church of England ritual from the ruins of Canterbury Cathedral in three thousand years' time.

Several small statuettes and part of a life-size stone figure have been found, all representing enormously fat women, with bulging arms and legs (Pl. 26). There are probably representations of the 'Mother Goddess', the goddess of fertility and plenty on whom the worshippers would have relied for the success of their harvests. Most of these statuettes had detachable heads and holes in the necks, through which cords could be led to make the goddess's head nod at her worshippers.

The carvings of animals probably represent the sacrifices which were offered to her. They would have been cut up by a flint knife like the one found at Hal Tarxien, and then placed in the holes behind the altars where animal remains have been discovered. Removable stone plugs in the floor may indicate where libations were poured. The pottery vessels used for this would then have been ceremonially broken, leaving us their useful evidence for dating.

All these ceremonies would have taken place in mounting awe, darkness, and secrecy. Holes specially carved in the stone in pairs to take screens and bars are very common at Hal Tarxien, and the innermost shrine of all is guarded by a stone barrier carved with two spirals like symbolic eyes staring out from the heart of the sanctuary (Pl. 22).

Professor Evans also showed me evidence of the activity of the priests who must have organized all this. A clay statuette broken in three pieces reveals the appearance of one. Square shoulders are set off by a long draped skirt which billows out slightly from the waist and then falls straight to the feet. His face, with a sharp straight nose, is serious, and his elaborate hair-style is a little like a modern barrister's wig.

One of the priests' duties seems to have been to occupy certain secret rooms hidden in the thickness of the walls. From here they could make objects appear mysteriously by a little concealed tunnel in one of the chambers of the temple, presumably as signs or portents. Other temples have small square openings seemingly leading into the rock, but in fact into other secret rooms, from which would come an apparently disembodied voice. This perhaps explains the significance of one of the most charming of all Maltese prehistoric objects, the six-inch long terracotta sleeping prophetess. She lies on her side on a curved wooden bed, dressed in a skirt, with one arm bent and head on her hand, rather like a Henry Moore sculpture in her ample curves. After an eerie night alone in the temple, she would emerge with her vision, her answer from the oracle, perhaps given by the disembodied voice of the priest. Did one, I wonder, ever foretell the disaster that was going to wipe out her people's civilization so completely? (Pl. 27).

I was particularly pleased to have gone to Malta, for reasons over and above the change from London slush to Mediterranean sun. As late as the summer of 1955, a book on the Etruscans by the well-known Italian historian, M. Pallotino, could begin, when listing the great unsolved problems of history, 'When and why did the ancient inhabitants of Malta raise the prodigious piles of their many Megalithic temples?'

Thanks to Professor Evans, we can very largely answer that question now. To go round filming the sites and the evidence with him, to tell the story in the programme almost in the hot flush of discovery, was a most exciting privilege. But for anyone interested in the past, Malta has advantages. Most famous prehistoric remains are solitary in their chance survival. If your interest is excited, you often have to travel a long way before you find something similar to help your understanding, and then that may have been affected by all sorts of different local circumstances.

Thanks to the several hundred peaceful years without invasion, the people who built the Maltese Megaliths were able to develop a particular local style that we can now follow from beginning to end. Professor

Evans has established the order, the dry sunny air has preserved nearly forty of them, the islands are so small that you can get to them all easily, and there is a lot of illustrative material to fill in the picture. There can be few better places to get an idea of the achievements and progress of a people at this stage of man's history.

D

CHAPTER VI

STONE AGE HOUSE-BUILDING

In the summer of 1953, Dr Daniel's influence and my increasing interest in archaeology led me to go on a dig in Anglesey, under the direction of Mr T. G. E. Powell and Dr Daniel. In the course of a week I removed about 120 barrow loads of earth from a stone-lined grave shaped like a cross, a so-called cruciform passage grave. It was energetic if you weren't used to it, but the sun shone, the site was delightfully placed on a headland covered with pink seathrift above the Irish Sea, and the under-graduates there worked much harder than I did. During that week we found nothing at all in the sense of buried treasure or objects of any sort, but every now and then to encourage us Dr Daniel would have another shot at deciphering the 'art'. This consisted of faint markings on the stones, and was the most important aspect of Barclodiad y Gawres, as the site was called. By wetting the stone and then chalking in the resulting dark lines you could make the designs look quite impressive. Amongst them were some spirals.

Prehistoric tombs with this decoration are rare in England and Wales. Hence the importance of Barclodiad. In Ireland, though, they are much more numerous, and there are some particularly fine examples in the great burial mound of New Grange.

When we were digging in Anglesey the connection between the spiral patterns there and those in the Maltese temples was uncertain, because at that time the date and origin of the Maltese examples were quite unknown. Now, thanks to Professor Evan's work in Malta, we can see both as part of a whole, the spread of an idea. These great stone monuments are one of the most impressive and important relics of ancient man. As such, we should sooner or later have had to include something about them in 'Buried Treasure' so I tried to discover from Dr Daniel and Séan P. Ó Ríordáin, Professor of Archaeology at University College, Dublin, what this idea was.

They explained that this practice of building great stone monuments and decorating them in a particular way probably started in the west

Mediterranean. From Malta it spread west and north by two routes, one across France and one round the coasts of Iberia. This does not mean that identical monuments are found in all these places, but burial chambers of great stones do appear here and there from Malta to the Irish Sea. All along the way, in Sardinia, Spain, France, Brittany, Ireland to the Orkneys and Denmark, the queer symbolic art of spirals and lozenges is found, sometimes on megaliths, sometimes on pottery. How and why this megalithic idea spread is a problem to archaeologists.

It has been described as a compelling religious idea. In other words, when some barbarous local tribe heard of this way of honouring their dead from more civilized visiting traders, they at once saw its point and adopted it themselves. On the other hand, megaliths also seem to be connected with the search for metal and follow the sea routes connected with this. Yet although they occur in areas that were rich in the newly appreciated copper and tin of this period, scarcely any metal tools are found in them. Perhaps it was all sent back home by the traders, or was too valuable to be buried with the dead.

Also, if these tombs were built for dominating traders with a higher level of civilization and a knowledge of metal, it is a problem how they managed to coerce the locals into such mighty labours, and what country had the energy and population to send out these persuasive pioneers. The answer is probably Mycenaean Greece and Crete, and if one is surprised at the distance from Crete to the west coast of Ireland and the small numbers that could have been carried by whatever skin or wood boats they used in Neolithic times, it seems to me that it is worth remembering what a superior technological level in weapons enabled a handful of Britons to achieve in India during the eighteenth century.

Anyway this megalithic idea reached Ireland either via Spain or across France, probably between 2,000 and 1,500 B.C. just as the Neolithic was becoming the Bronze Age. No definite date can be given for this moment, of course. There are all sorts of complications, but generally speaking the further away from the Eastern Mediterranean the later the Bronze Age starts.

Ireland at this time was not only a rich source of metals but was also not shut off by any great physical obstacles in the shape of mountain ranges or great forests. Consequently megaliths are numerous and widely scattered. There are about two thousand altogether in the British Isles. For details of the controversy as to how they should be classified you must read the relevant authorities. In Professor Stuart Piggott's *Neolithic Cultures of the British Isles*, in Dr Daniel's *Prehistoric Chamber Tombs of England and Wales*, and in Professor Séan Ó Riórdaín's *Antiquities of the*

Irish Countryside, the various possibilities are set out. In them you can learn about the mysteries of orthostats, peristaliths, southern wedge-shaped galleries, and morphological classification. I will not go beyond saying that there are two main types, the passage grave and the gallery grave, on which we concentrated when we decided to do a programme about these imposing remains of prehistoric man in which Ireland is so rich.

Gallery graves are long structures built of stone slabs, generally 5 to 6 feet high. Their builders seem originally to have come from the south of France and the Pyrenees. Sometimes they are divided into compartments by slabs called septals, with portholes in them which some people consider were made to let out the spirits of the dead. The one we filmed at Knockcurraboola, in Tipperary, had a fine position. We reached it through a lonely farmyard in the centre of Ireland. It stood on a little bare rise behind the farm, commanding a wild sweep of valley, with hardly a building of any sort in sight for miles, its sidestones sticking up like a blunt row of teeth where the roofing had fallen.

Even more impressive are the great mounds of the passage graves near the River Boyne. There is a group of them here, but the most famous is New Grange. This great pyramid of the West is 240 feet in diameter, and 45 feet high. Today its profile has been slightly damaged by the removal of some of its mound, but its original architect must have had grandiose ideas. Round the outer edge was a circle of standing stones. The mound itself had a kerb of stones round its base, three of which were elaborately carved and decorated, while the main part consisted of loose boulders and small stones. Some of these are of whitish quartz brought from some way away. It is possible that the mound was originally covered with these, and early descriptions seem to show it had a single pillar on its top.

Imagine it then, as it first was, a huge, sparkling white mound, crowned by a pillar, surrounded by its circle of great stones, standing up on its hill, dominating the bend of the River Boyne.

To reach the burial chamber inside the mound you have to go along a passage 60 feet long. This is lined and roofed with great slabs of stone, many of them decorated with the spirals, diamonds, and lines of megalithic art. At one place the stones lean in so much that you have to go down on all fours to get by. The passage has slight curves in it too, so that you soon lose the daylight from the entrance (Pl. 30).

Eventually you come to the burial chamber, with its great corbelled roof, the finest in north-west Europe. Corbelling is a method of roofing an open space by starting at the edges with slabs of stone laid flat, then putting the next layer on top slightly closer in, all the while preventing them tipping inwards and holding them in position by covering their outer edges with boulders. As the layers rise, they get closer together until finally they almost meet and a single slab will cover the remaining gap.

The corbelled roof at New Grange rises to a height of over 19 feet and covers an area about 12 feet across. It has stood untouched and un-repaired, without mortar of any sort, supporting the tons of weight of the mound above, for over three thousand years, a wonderful tribute to the skill of its builders.

The chamber itself is in the shape of a cross, with three cells leading off the central area. These probably each contained a large stone basin about 4 feet across, on which the remains of the dead were placed in bags, fastened with pins of bone. Now two of the basins are on top of each other in one of the cells, and one of the other cells is without one.

All the cells are decorated but the one with the two basins in it has a particularly fine flat roof, a stone covered with all sorts of designs, in particular two series of concentric circles with a line in between which may be a stylized representation of the eyes and nose of the Mother Goddess. To appreciate this properly, you have to risk rheumatics and lie on your back on the chilly stone basin, but it is worth it. (Pl. 31.)

As you lie there, looking at these mysterious signs, it is worth trying to imagine what strange scenes lie behind them, the labour of pocking the stones with sharp-pointed pieces of quartz, the effort it must have cost these herdsmen and farmers to build that mound, and the eerie scene as the thick black silence was broken by the scrape of bodies and feet along the passage and the smoky patterns of light from torches as the remains of some great king were laid to rest.

These Irish monuments share another characteristic with those of Malta. Very little is known about the homes of the people who built them. There is one fairly obvious reason for this. They probably chose the best sites for their houses, and people have gone on living there ever since. This is particularly so in Malta, where there is very little room anyway. The parish priests' house in Zurriq, for instance, consists partly of a Phoenician or early Roman house, and most of the foundations of the megalith-builders' homes have probably suffered the same sort of fate. They lie under the foundations of modern houses.

It is also a question of archaeological technique. The earliest method was to go and get what you could out of some convenient burial mound. The next step was towards a more scientific examination of burials, temples, and so on, taking into account all available evidence of dating, type, and origin, etc. Finally, with the evolution of the type of skills described by Sir Mortimer Wheeler in *Archaeology from the Earth* it became possible to make something of the faint remains of prehistoric homes. These are usually marked only by the changed colouration of the earth where wooden poles or brushwood walls once stood, sometimes slight mounds over foundations, and ashes in the earth where there was once a hearth.

The odds against anyone finding a hoard of treasure are tremendous. But if as an amateur archaeologist you find an undisturbed settlement site, of which there must be many undiscovered, you will be very popular with the professionals.

This accounts for the importance of the Lough Gur site. Lough Gur is a lake in south-west Ireland, into which juts the high rocky peninsula of Knockadoon, one of a group of limestone hills in the neighbourhood. To the south are the mountains on the County Cork border. All around is the plain of Limerick. Two mediaeval castles guard the marshy neck of the peninsula.

In 1939 some shallow stones on the south face of Knockadoon turned out, on excavation, to mark the remains of a house. Further investigation showed that there were a number of these house sites there, whose occupation had lasted from the Neolithic to the Bronze Age.

With such a lovely setting for a dig, who can blame Professor Ó Ríordáin for working there most summers from then until 1955. Besides, this was one of the few good settlement sites known in north-west Europe, and the only one in Ireland.

In his reports, he describes why the early Neolithic farmers picked on Knockadoon. Its pleasant southern aspect, good drainage, light soil as compared with the heavier Limerick plain soil, and plentiful supply of water would all have appealed to them.

Evidence of the popularity of the site is abundant. Amongst the many remains there is a gallery grave just across the lake, and one of the several stone circles nearby is particularly fine. This is the stone circle of Grange. It consists of a 30-foot wide bank against which stand great stones side by side all the way round. It is 150 feet across, and some of the stones are thick 50-ton monsters. Excavation proved clearly that it was used for some form of worship, not as an enclosed living place, and as with many other sites nearby the pottery used for purposes of worship turned out to be much finer than that used domestically.

But it is the houses on Knockadoon that are really important. When Professor Ó Ríordáin suggested building one, based on all the information that had been obtained from excavation, I was delighted. The trouble with megaliths is that they are an extremely static subject. To hold the attention, a film subject must move, and have some sense of suspense about it. There is a limit to what can be done by changing the camera shot, or having someone walk round the subject. All architecture suffers from this disadvantage. A house being built or a site being excavated is a far better subject for filming than the finished house or revealed ruin.

Now a possible solution to our particular problem had appeared. We could give the first part of the programme up to a straightforward architectural record of New Grange and a representative selection of other types of Irish megaliths; then in the second part of the programme we could move on to what was known of the domestic life of the megalith builders. This would bring in the putting-up of the house, which would have all the movement and occurrence on which television thrives, as well as being a small but interesting archaeological experiment.

The basis of the house was the plan of one of the excavated ones. The material was to consist only of what would have been available to Stone Age man. The actual structure of course was guesswork, though a great deal of care was taken by Mr John Hunt, who directed the actual building, to make every possible use of the available evidence.

We began by cutting down a small tree with a polished stone axe-head, which was found in a local garden, mounted in a modern haft. I often wish the film we took of this could be seen in a little box beside every museum case containing a polished stone axe. My own reactions in the past had been, at the most, 'polished stone—Neolithic—queer fat shape—suppose they knew what they were doing.' It really surprised me how effective it was. It cut down the tree without any trouble. Of course, the wood was young and green; on dry, hard timber it would have been useless. One man, quite easily, had the trunk ready for trimming in just a few minutes. All the posts of the house were not made this way, needless to say. We were satisfied once we had established that it was feasible for the original habitants to have made posts like this.

The same went for the ropes used for tying the rafters and roof-beams to the supporting posts. For these we used sugans, ropes made of twisted rushes. To see them being made was fascinating. One man twisted some round a stick then, twirling the stick in his right hand, fed in more rushes given him by another man on his left. As more and more rushes were fed in, the sugan grew larger and longer, and the man feeding in the rushes moved further away from the stick-twirler. Once we had made enough sugans to prove they were competent for their purpose, we reverted to rope.

Having no nails, the Neolithic house-builders would have had to tie on all their roof-beams and rafters. No remains of a roof existed, but it would certainly have been sloping to throw off the rain, which was doubtless as prevalent then as when it held up our filming for a day and a half. For the rest, Professor Ó Ríordáin had to deduce what he could from the ground plan of the post-holes of the house which we had chosen as our model. There were forty-one, between 7 and 10 inches in diameter, in a double row round the outer walls and two internal rows. They were probably dug in the soft ground by the tine of a deer's antlers, used as a pick. These antler picks were very common in this period. You will hear about them at Stonehenge and many have been found in Neolithic flint mines like Grimes Graves in Norfolk. Some of the holes then had small stones put in them as a support to the post.

The plan of the house was oblong, some 32 feet long by 20 feet wide, with a 3-foot wide doorway in one corner. Mr Hunt tied beams across the top of the posts, and then with rafters on those made a sloping base onto which bundles of reeds from the nearby marsh were tied as thatch.

The irregular stones of the sides, which first drew attention to the houses, were not suitable for the building of a proper wall. They were too tumbled and haphazard. Their purpose must have been to mark the line of the wall, act as a foundation, and help the drainage.

Whatever was then placed on top left no trace, so it was probably not clay. Reeds, brushwood, or turf are more likely, and they would have been held in place by the pairs of posts on each side. We used a layer of turf on top of the stones, and then bundles of reeds.

Mr Hunt took particular care to choose a part of the hillside with exactly the same slope as on the original site. The result was that at the back the thatch practically came down to the hillside and the whole effect was very snug (Pl. 28).

I got two impressions from it, which I hope also came across in the programme. One was how well it fitted into the landscape. It looked right, and not like a strange or alien imposition. Secondly, it recalled many pictures of African huts and houses. Presumably the methods and materials of those differ very little.

Inside it was dry, warm, and comfortable, and experience proved it stood up to the weather very well.

There were three other typical features which I have not said anything about, a hearth for a fire, a pit for rubbish, and a small patch of flat stones, a sort of table, on the trampled earth.

One of the casualties of archaeology has been the idea of a Golden Age, an innocent Spring in the history of Man. The Neolithic and Bronze Age inhabitants of Lough Gur are perhaps the nearest one could get to this. Professor Ó Ríordáin saw no signs of warfare survive amongst their remains. The scenery must have been as beautiful and the climate as gentle

28 & 29. ABOVE. A reconstruction of a Stone Age house at Lough Gur in Ireland, specially built for our 'Buried Treasure' programme. BELOW. The interior of the Stone Age house.

30 & 31. ABOVE. Glyn Daniel and Séan Ó Ríordáin looking at one of the stones decorated with megalithic art in the 60-foot-long passage way that leads to the burial chambers in the great mound of New Grange in Ireland. BELOW. The carved roof of one of the side chambers of New Grange. Just above the big spiral is a motif which some people think is a stylized human face.

32 & 33. ABOVE. The West Kennet long barrow before excavation. BELOW. Televising an excavation actually in progress. Building a ramp for a television camera alongside the excavated chambers of the West Kennet long barrow. In the background are one of the lights and some of the television control vehicles.

34. Professor Stuart Piggott unearthing a large piece of Peterborough pottery found by the author in the forecourt blocking of the West Kennet long barrow. The edge of the piece of pottery is just beginning to show beyond the point of the trowel.

35 & 36. ABOVE. Problems of a producer. The author, centre of the group of three in the foreground, discusses with Professor Piggott (left) and Dr Daniel (right) some of the problems of the television broadcast from the West Kennet long barrow. Part of one of the cameras is visible on the horizon and another is just out of sight in the actual passage of the tomb to the right. BELOW. Sir Mortimer Wheeler and Dr Glyn Daniel during filming of one of the Brittany cliff castles.

37. Aerial view of Stonehenge.

38. An experiment in hauling a copy of one of the bluestones, which were brought to Stonehenge from Wales in prehistoric times.

39 & 40. ABOVE. Lowering the copy of a Stonehenge bluestone on to a possible reconstruction of a neolithic craft. BELOW. The copy of a Stonehenge bluestone being punted up the Avon.

in their day as in ours. Terraces show they did cultivate the light soil a little but cattle were their main support. Remains of red deer, fish, and birds like duck, sea eagle, goose, crane, and teal indicate what they hunted, but it cannot have been a vital source of food. Bear, of which there is very scanty evidence, seems to have been the only serious danger.

Boredom, which might also have assailed a small isolated community, would have been lightened by the frequent comings and goings. The changing styles of pottery reflect the influence of outside people and ideas. The porcellanite axes from County Antrim, a little gold disc, and the bronze cast in the moulds, all imply that the early inhabitants of Lough Gur had some trading contacts.

Perhaps most remarkable are the glass beads. These are small rings, greenish blue in colour, which were made by winding the molten glass round a wire, and then chipping off the beads when it had cooled. The Lough Gur beads are very like some found at Abydos in Egypt which date from about 1400 B.C. Perhaps the Lough Gur ones came from the Continent, round the necks of the megalith builders themselves, as they cautiously coasted from point to point, skimming over the big Atlantic seas in skin boats like umiaks, the women's boats of the Eskimos.

To me, the boat question is one of the most fascinating problems presented by these people. Just what sort of craft did they use? Even going from point to point in the finest weather, the Atlantic off the west coast of Ireland can be dangerous to small craft. All you can say definitely is that the Continental origins and associations of these people are unmistakable, so they must have crossed the Channel and the Irish Sea at least.

Expert opinion in Scandinavia is moving away from the traditional dug-out theory towards skin boats. Certainly dug-outs, which are usually assumed to be the main ancestor of western european boats, are not very good in big seas. On the other hand the Eskimos' skin boats ride the seas in a remarkable way. Kayaks have even been reported off Scotland, blown there possibly from the Faeroes or Iceland. Boats shown in Stone Age Scandinavian paintings are believed to be skin-built.

But however they got there, the early inhabitants of Lough Gur, in their snug reed houses on the gentle slopes of Knockadoon, would have had good reason to agree with the old sailor's saying 'a passage perilous makyth a port pleasant'.

CHAPTER VII

THE WEST KENNET
LONG BARROW

IN THE SUMMER of 1954 I drove back to Kent from a holiday in North Devon by the Bath Road. Just outside Marlborough I stopped to climb Silbury Hill, the strange, flat-topped hump that was the largest artificial mound in Europe before the Industrial Revolution. A little further on across the road was a stile and a Ministry of Works notice that pointed the way to the West Kennet long barrow.

After a quarter of a mile walk up a slight hill, I came to the site. It did not look very exciting on a dull September evening, a long, untidy mound half hidden in a bristle of weeds and long grass. At one end a scatter of large stones lay flat on the ground in no pattern that one could understand. Only two or three stumps sticking out seemed to hint at some sort of a ceremonial entrance (Pl. 32).

Nevertheless, I looked at it with considerable attention. We had always wanted to do a programme from an excavation actually in progress, from the moment the 'Buried Treasure' programmes started being a success. This seemed the most likely answer.

Professor Stuart Piggott and Mr Richard Atkinson, respectively Professor and Lecturer in Prehistoric Archaeology at Edinburgh University, were going to do the excavation. They were willing to allow the broadcast, and so were the Ministry of Works. Dates and the availability of a television outside broadcast unit also fitted.

In this way I found myself getting to know the site very much better the following summer. Professor Piggott very kindly agreed to put up with an inexperienced volunteer, I had a week's leave to spare, and the programme was planned as the early stages of the excavation took place.

It was very different from the previous dig which I had been on at Barclodiad. Like most well-known barrows the West Kennet one had been dug in the nineteenth century, when archaeology was largely a matter of plunder. Fortunately, it turned out in this case that Thurnam, who had burrowed into the main chamber in 1859, had missed four side chambers. These were therefore waiting untouched and full of promise for the skilled attention and modern methods of the excavators from Edinburgh.

By the time I got there, much of the turf had been removed and the shape of the structure was much clearer. The actual burial chambers occupied only the eastern part of the 350-foot long mound. There were five of them, leading off a central passage, roughly in the shape of a cross of Lorraine, that is to say, two each side and one at the head. The chambers and passage were built of great, rough, unworked sarsen stones, and had originally been covered by large capstones, on top of which the earth of the mound had been piled.

Across the front of the mound was a curving façade of standing stones with an entrance in the middle. Just what had happened to the entrance was one of the problems that the excavation hoped to solve.

The skilled hands of the party, in this case all girls, worked on the chambers, delicately skimming off the filling, layer by layer. The others, including myself, did the rougher work of clearing square sections across the entrance, while all the time Professor Piggott and Mr Atkinson plotted, recorded, pondered, and advised.

It is hard to explain the pleasure of that week. We stayed in a pub in Avebury, the village in the centre of the great stone circle, which was appropriate enough. Its beer and roast beef, after a day's digging, were incomparable.

The site itself was on a bare shoulder of the Marlborough Downs, the dark rim of the Wansdyke along one horizon, Silbury Hill cutting the other, clumps of trees, a church-tower, and all around a great wheel of sun, and sky, and downland.

It was hard work to anyone used to an office chair, but never for a moment boring, as the shape emerged beneath pick and trowel, and every solution was salted with new problems. Unlike Barclodiad, there was no lack of finds. Scarcely an hour seemed to pass without something emerging. To crown my own particular pleasure, I actually uncovered an object. As an untrained volunteer clearing the blocking in the façade, I had no expectations of this, but apparently some bones and a pot must have been dropped there. Professor Piggott thinks this may have happened when the contents of the burial chambers were being removed or robbed. Perhaps removing the bones was part of some superstitious activity, like placing human finger bones in the crevices between the stones in the main chamber. One cannot tell.

Anyway my discovery was first a small piece of pottery, then a very large piece, almost a quarter of a pot, with a human femur just by it. Many television programmes are described as museum pieces, but I think I must be the first producer to contribute an actual specimen to a museum in the course of his work.

Most of the finds appeared in the chambers, were plotted, catalogued, and if of any importance, photographed *in situ* before being removed. Such an excavation is in fact a destruction of evidence, unless everything is carefully recorded. However insignificant some small find seems at the time, it may be the vital clue in some new problem that arises later on.

Most of the finds consisted of animal bones, bone tools and pins, flint tools, ornaments and beads of bone and stone, pottery, and then on the original floor level of the chambers, the bodies for whose burial the tomb was built. As in the Maltese megaliths, the pieces of pottery were vital for dating the various stages of the barrow's development.

There were three main types of pottery which even I was beginning to recognize by the end of the dig, Windmill Hill, Peterborough, and Beaker. These are all connected with important events in the early history of Britain.

At a date which pre-historians argue about, approximately 2000 B.C. or a little earlier, Professor Piggott explained that the scattered bands of hunters and fishermen who were then the inhabitants of Britain began to feel the impact of the invasion from France of peasant farmers who were the heralds of the Neolithic revolution.

The first Neolithic invaders are known as the Windmill Hill people, from their best known site near Avebury. They brought with them cattle, corn, pottery, and polished stone axes to make clearings in the forest. In his *Neolithic Cultures of the British Isles* Professor Piggott has described the scenes that must have taken place in their camps, like that of Windmill Hill, with its concentric rings of ditches and the gaps or causeways between them, where the cattle would have been driven in for the autumn round-up and the slaughter which lack of winter fodder necessitated.

'There, for some days or weeks, the tribes from round about would camp, roasting joints of veal in the lee of the enclosure banks, milking cows into the bowls carried up from the village, perhaps making cheese. To the men would doubtless fall the tasks of the cow-boy and the butcher, but to the women the preparation of the skins of the calves and the tougher hides of the grown animals and the conversion of some into new leather clothing against the coming winter.' This communal existence also made possible another practice which they had brought with them from north-west France, the burial of their dead in great, earthen long barrows.

The earliest Neolithic inhabitants of Lough Gur probably were roughly contemporary with the Windmill Hill people, and both have claims on our respect. With their little scratched corn plots, their clearings in the forest, their camps and burial mounds, they were the first people to modify the face of Britain and Ireland, to scar nature's efforts with the handiwork of man and start creating the landscape that is so familiar today.

Soon afterwards both peoples were joined by other invaders, probably from further west in France. These people had more sophisticated ideas about burial. They placed their dead in chambered tombs built of rough stone into long earthen mounds, and what is more, used them as a sort of family vault, placing more and more bodies in them over the years until finally for some reason they ceased to be used and were sealed up for good. These tomb-builders belonged to the Severn-Cotswold culture which produced the West Kennet long barrow itself, as well as Hetty Pegler's Tump, Wayland's Smithy, and many other well-known tombs. They were in fact the first of the megalith builders to reach Britain, in the course of the long journey of the practice from the Mediterranean to Scandinavia.

Yet another invasion, a little later, arrived in the East, probably from across the North Sea. These people combined very rapidly with survivors of the old hunter and fisher people, and from the give and take of ideas formed a new culture, which is called after the Peterborough site. While breeding cattle and making pottery, they led a life more like that of their hunting and fishing predecessors, and their wanderings were probably encouraged by their exploitation of the flint trade. They were responsible for most of the flint mines, like Grimes Graves, and stone axe factories, like Great Langdale, which are one of the more remarkable features of the period.

Their pottery is coarser than that of the Windmill Hill people, and more decorated. These decorations were made by pressing bird bones, fingernails, shells, and cord into the clay. It was quite fascinating to watch Professor Piggott imitating the pattern on one piece of pottery found at West Kennet by pressing a chicken bone into a sheet of plasticine.

The next important invasion, one of the many of which the early history of Britain is so largely made up, was by the Beaker folk. They may have introduced the Bronze Age to Britain. They were a vigorous, warlike people, whose travels took them from Spain through France to Britain and to north Italy, and from there via central Europe and the Rhine back to Britain. In our islands they have left traces from Sussex to the west of Ireland and the Orkneys.

Such was the strength and coherence of their character and traditions that their pottery, the tall-waisted beakers with patterned lines from which their name comes, is recognizably identical in all the sites of their wanderings.

They were not great metal-workers themselves, but they did bring the first simple metal tools to Britain about 1,700 B.C., as well as the first gold ornaments and the practice of burying their dead singly under round barrows.

This is the barest possible outline of a complicated and vital stage in our history, as learnt from Professor Piggott in the intervals of the excavation.

I put it in to show some of the implications of the bits of pottery, seemingly so grubby and irrelevant, which came out of the West Kennet long barrow. Their relationship in the various levels to each other could reveal much of the time-scale of the tomb's history, and the different people who used it at different times. Of all the interesting activities involved in that dig, I enjoyed most hearing the two archaeologists in charge weighing up the various pieces of evidence, from a piece of pottery to the disturbance of a patch of earth, testing the possibilities, reading so much from what not only appeared meaningless but what was easy not to see at all, until it was pointed out to you.

For instance in one of the chambers, about half way down through the layers of the filling, there appeared a very fine specimen of a beaker upside down in a corner. Did this, and the various other finds, wood ash, pottery, tools and so on, that appeared in the higher levels mean that after its original use as a tomb a later group of people came and lived in it, sleeping and eating above the bodies that were its first occupants? Or had the filling of the chambers been put there for some incomprehensible ritual reason? Were there signs that the entrance had been blocked and then deliberately broken into, or had the blocking stone fallen of its own accord? To hear the problems discussed, and see the evidence being revealed, layer after layer by the delicate scrape of a trowel, made the best detective story tame in comparison.

I always regretted that I did not succeed in putting over this feeling of excitement in the programme. In fact I did persuade Professor Piggott to let some excavation take place during the transmission and some pottery did appear, while we were on the air, where it should not have done but, as Mr Atkinson said very reasonably afterwards, he was certainly not going to archaeologize in those circumstances.

It was also, of course, too early to include in the programme any deductions from the anatomist's examination of the bones of the twenty to thirty bodies of the men, women, and children who were discovered in the tomb. But, judging by other similar chambered tombs, the evidence may show whether all the burials had some physical peculiarity that indicated they belonged to the same family, or whether earlier burials were packed away as, over a long period of time, new ones were added. The jaws may show that the unfortunate owners only rarely suffered from dental decay but often from 'dirt pyorrhoea', an unpleasant infection of the gums. Other bones may show the presence of arthritis. The bending of the bones of the toes may hint at the wearing of sandals.

Another piece of evidence that did not appear was that of a trepanned skull. Quite improperly from the archaeological point of view, I longed loudly and publicly for one, because it would have made such excellent programme material.

Five skulls are known in Britain that show signs of this extraordinary practice. All are probably Bronze Age in date, though there are several Stone Age examples known in Europe. One man even survived four rings being cut out of his skull before he died when the fifth was being removed. It is possible to tell this from the state of the edge of the cut bore. Apparently this method was to wear away a circle in the bone by moving a sharp flint round and round until the ring of bone in the centre could be levered out. One cannot conceive that any headache, and presumably the object was to relieve an imagined pressure on the brain, would justify the horrors of such an operation, but that is another problem about our remote ancestors to which we shall never have an answer.

The absence of trepanned skulls and other difficulties notwithstanding, I still think the programme was a remarkable event in its way. I blushed frequently as I saw what I had inflicted on the excavators, the masses of cars, the vans, the aerials and lights, the crowds held back by policemen, the staging for the cameras over the excavation, the generator humming, and even a camera trundling along the passage of the tomb itself. As one harassed archaeologist said, it only needed a steam organ to make it more like a fair than an excavation.

Yet, after all, most excavation today depends on public money and here was the best possible propaganda for it, a very important dig brought to the attention of millions while it was actually happening. I hope, too, that it will have encouraged people to come and see the West Kennet long barrow.

To the visitor, when the Ministry of Works have made safe and opened up this monument, it will be the largest and finest of its kind in England. Even if the 350-foot mound is less high than originally, the façade and forecourt are battered, and its core of piled boulders and deep flanking ditches stay hidden under the earth, the great sarsen boulders from the valley, the 8-foot high passage under the capstones, and mysterious corbelled side-chambers make it impressive enough. When you think as well of the first farmers four thousand years ago, with their arthritis and septic mouths, their sandals and skin clothes, leaving their herds on the chalky uplands to haul these great boulders up the hill from the valley and build a great tomb and then after a funeral feast of ceremonially roast oxen, tempered perhaps with beer, or milk, or cheese, or even porridge, laying to rest the body of some ruler with his flint knife and bone pendants or a little child princess with her pathetic ring of stone beads, then this early example of English monumental architecture surely becomes worth a visit.

CHAPTER VIII

STONEHENGE

OF ALL THE FAMOUS ancient monuments I know, Stonehenge can be least impressive at first sight. Lascaux, New Grange, Avebury, all survive crowds, guides, lights, and notices and keep an inward remoteness that moves the imagination. Stonehenge, with its crowds, its over-tidy grass, the road running practically through it, the car park and kiosk, the rash of pink bungalows across the valley, can look like a cardboard stage set of an obviousness and familiarity that is quite disillusioning.

I was fortunate enough to see it for the first time early in the war in the days of petrol-rationing. I had bicycled over from Warminster on a hot summer's morning and there was nobody else there at all. I knew nothing about it then, but the feeling of something strange and strong, quite incomprehensible and yet forcing itself on your attention because of its sheer lasting power, was very compelling. I have never felt anything like that the many times I have visited it since. Perhaps it is knowing more about it or perhaps it is just that the first impression can have such an effect. I little thought then that I would one day be in charge of a programme that would bring the latest knowledge about it to the attention of millions.

I began this programme by asking Professor Piggott to explain the shape of the monument. The limits, he said, are marked by a ditch, forming a circle about 100 yards in diameter. On both sides, though larger on the inside, there is a bank made of the chalk rubble thrown up from the ditch. Into this runs, on the north-east, the Avenue, which is a two-mile ceremonial way winding up from the River Avon, marked by a ditch on each side. This gives the whole thing a frying pan shape. The heelstone, a single rough sarsen, a natural sandstone boulder, stands in the Avenue just outside the entrance, like a rivet in the frying pan handle (Pl. 37).

Inside the bank and ditch are fifty-six pits, about 3 feet deep, called Aubrey holes, after the seventeenth-century antiquary. Cremated human bones have been found in some of these and in various other parts of the ditch and bank.

E

Moving inwards still, you come next to a ring, about 100 feet across, of carefully worked sarsens about 15 feet high, with what was originally a continuous ring of lintel stones on top of them. These contain some of the most remarkable architectural features of the whole monument. The 7-ton lintels, which are curved in shape to fit the circle, are joined to each other by a tongue and groove worked in each alternate stone. Each one, too, has two mortices (hollows) on its underside, which fit over tenons (projections) on top of the uprights. It is generally considered that these forms are basically those used in working wood. Stonehenge may therefore be partly a great copy in stone of an earlier wooden monument, like the one that stood at Woodhenge nearby. This is a circle of holes which once held timber uprights inside a ditch and bank.

Inside the sarsen circle of Stonehenge is another circle of single, much smaller, stones, the bluestones, so called from their bluish colour. Some of these have odd grooves and holes worked in them, showing they were at one time used in some more elaborate way than standing as single stones. Inside the remains of the ring of bluestones are five sarsen trilithons standing in a horseshoe shape. These trilithons (the word comes from the Greek 'three stones'), consist of two uprights with a single lintel stone across the top. Inside the trilithons again is another horseshoe of single upright bluestones. Finally, inside that is a single sarsen lying on the ground, the so-called altar stone. The horseshoe settings face the avenue and are aligned so that the rays of the rising sun on Midsummer's Day strike along the axis.

The legend that this was a signal for a human sacrifice to be made on the altar stone was quite deflated by Professor Piggott. The altar stone is just a fallen upright, one of a pair that probably marked the alignment on the rising sun.

The size of the trilithons is extraordinarily impressive. The uprights are over 20 feet high and weigh up to 80 tons. The lintels are attached by the same mortice and tenon method, and in addition they slope up towards the outside edge to counteract the foreshortening effect which you get when looking at them from the ground.

One of the fallen sarsens, whose dressing is half finished, shows very well how the great stones were smoothed and worked into such accurate shapes. Mr Atkinson demonstrated how they were pounded into parallel grooves by round balls of stone, used as mauls, and then the ridges in between were in turn pounded down. Many of these pounding-stones have been found. They fit very neatly into the grooves on the unfinished sarsen. Some are rather larger than a cricket ball, and can be held and wielded in the hand quite easily. Others are a little larger than a football, and it is very hard work continuously lifting them up in both hands and then dropping them onto the surface to be smoothed. It is the only way, though, that this could be done, for the sarsens are so hard that they will turn the blade of any but the most modern steel tool. Mr Atkinson calculates it would take two men working full time for two months to smooth a surface of one of the large sarsens and that it would have taken fifty masons, working ten hours a day, seven days a week, nearly three years to dress all the sarsens.

Others of the uprights have places where the smooth stripes that finally resulted are still left unweathered, so that you can run your hand over them and feel the finish which the ancient stone-masons achieved. Finally most of the sarsen faces looking inward were polished by grinding.

The other great achievement of the builders of Stonehenge is the raising of the stones into position, and this is where our programme on Stonehenge really started to flourish. The dating, the architectural details, and the various stages of the monument Mr Atkinson and Professor Piggott described with models of Stonehenge from Salisbury Museum, and film, and very agreeably they did it too, after a little bullying from me on the subject of not using too technical language. But when we came to the specially made working models showing how the stones and lintels were raised, the programme gained one of those moments of fascinating revelation which one always strives for and so rarely gets. Television produces few memorable phrases. It is the occasional situation or picture that stays in the mind. I can still see exactly how those models looked on the screen. The method used to raise the uprights, which Mr Atkinson demonstrated with them, is reasonably clear.

First, a pit was dug with antler picks. This would have one side upright and the other sloping at a shallow angle. The upright side of the pit would then be lined with freshly-peeled palings. These would protect this side of the pit from the foot of the great stone, which would be moved towards the other side of the pit on rollers. At the critical moment, when its centre of gravity passed the lip of the sloping edge, the stone would tip down and its foot would come to rest in the bottom of the pit up against the palings. The whole stone would then be lying along the sloping edge of the pit. To pull it up, a rope, or several ropes, made of hides, would be attached to the top of the stone. This would lead to a pair of sheerlegs, and from there a rope would go to the hauling party of perhaps a hundred or two hundred men. The object of the sheerlegs would be to get a pull at right angles to the stone (Frontispiece).

As the stone was hauled upright its toe would slide easily down on the fresh-peeled palings, which would also prevent it damaging the side of the pit. As soon as the stone was upright, the rest of the pit on the sloping side would be hastily filled in to hold it in position, anything to hand being thrown in, including the mauls which had been used to smooth it. The pits, the palings, and the mauls have all been confirmed by excavation.

What is much more uncertain is how the lintels were raised onto the uprights. Our model demonstrated one method, the sloping ramp. This was built of timber, in theory, round the two uprights, with one side sloping down fairly gently. Ropes would then be led from the opposite side over the top of the uprights, down the slope of the ramp, round the lintel waiting at its foot, back up the ramp, and over the uprights to the hauling party on the other side. When they heaved away, the lintel would be pulled up the ramp, turning over and over until it had rolled up to the platform at the top. There the mortices and tenons would be adjusted and it would be levered into its final position. The timber ramp would then be dismantled ready for use on the next one.

It was fascinating to watch on the model the lintel rolling over and over so neatly and convincingly. The trouble is that the ramps would probably have left traces in the ground and none has appeared in excavation.

Mr Atkinson has another theory which was suggested to him by a timber expert from the Burmese teak forests. There, apparently, they have a method of raising large weights by building up a platform of logs under them, layer by layer, levering the weight up first from one side, then from the other, as the platform rises. The timber expert said that raising the 15-ton lintels would be no problem with this method.

Whatever method was used, one can appreciate what a tremendous and elaborate work Stonehenge was, and with what brilliant accuracy its plan and level were laid out. West Kennet, New Grange, and Avebury impress by their size and the labour that must have gone into them. Stonehenge represents something more. Whatever architect, priest, or king conceived it must have had a spectacular imagination, great driving power, skilful organization, and impressive technical ability. No wonder it is unique in the world. Whether or not you gain any sense of atmosphere from it, you can still admire it as an achievement.

Thanks to the work of Professor Stuart Piggott, Mr Richard Atkinson, and Dr J. F. S. Stone between 1950 and 1954, we now have a good idea of the stages and dates by which the final form was reached.

The earliest part was the bank, ditch, heelstone, and Aubrey holes. The objects found in these were typical of the later Neolithic peoples of southern England, the makers of Peterborough pottery, as opposed to the early ones who built the West Kennet long barrow. This gives a date of about 1700 B.C. which was in fact supported by carbon 14 dating of some charcoal from an Aubrey hole.

Very soon after the earliest stage the Avenue was added and the first bluestone monument was put up. The 1954 excavations revealed that this consisted of two rings of eighty-two stones in all, with the inner circle very close to the outer. The discovery of the traces of this early bluestone monument was in fact first announced publicly in our programme on Stonehenge.

One of the most intriguing points about Stonehenge is that the rock of which the bluestones consist is found only in the Prescelly Hills in Pembrokeshire. When I was planning the programme I was delighted to discover that no one had ever tried to see how difficult it would have been to move a bluestone the 180 miles or so from Pembrokeshire to Wiltshire. With the help of Mr Atkinson and Professor Piggott I therefore organized a practical experiment in the hope that it would make a good subject for filming, like the building of the Stone Age house.

Here was an ideal chance for television. A practical experiment would have all the drama and movement of an actual event, and the results would be intriguing to viewers and archaeologists alike.

Mr Atkinson drew plans of a raft of dug-outs and a wooden sledge, a local contractor made the copy of a bluestone in concrete and the raft, our Scenery Department made the sledge, and we eventually got them all together at Stonehenge. For the slave labour I had what I considered a brilliant idea. I asked the headmasters of Bryanston and Canford schools if they would let their senior boys take part in an experiment in practical education with some hard pulling attached. They agreed and all was ready for filming.

The raft was made of three dug-outs with a platform on top.

Dug-outs not being easily available, we used punt-shaped boxes, which in fact were inferior in strength to dug-outs but were otherwise similar enough for our purposes. The complete structure was some 18 feet long, 7 feet 6 inches wide, and drew 9 inches with the bluestone aboard. It was an exciting moment as a hired crane gently lowered the copied bluestone onto the platform of the craft, which we had moored to a bank of the Avon just outside Salisbury. To our relief, the craft neither sank, broke up, nor grounded, and was soon under way, moving very easily upstream or down under the thrust of four punt poles wielded by volunteers from Bryanston. With half a dozen people towing it from the bank, and one aboard to steer, it moved even more impressively. I think all concerned were surprised how easy it was. There might not have been solid well-defined banks in those days from which it was feasible to do the towing, and getting the stone on board might have been quite complicated, but otherwise the river-borne part of the operation would not have been too difficult. At sea, Mr Atkinson thinks the stone might have been carried underneath the raft. There would have been no danger of grounding, and the stability would have been much better. Even so, I don't know that our craft would have been seaworthy (Pl. 40).

That inclines me to support the more inland of the two most likely routes by which the stones might have come to Stonehenge. One is from Milford Haven round Land's End, along the south coast and up the Hampshire Avon. The other, which I think much more probable, is round the north shore of the Bristol Channel, up the Somersetshire Avon, overland to the headwaters on the Wylye, down to the junction with the Avon, and then up that to the point two miles from Stonehenge. Finally they may have been dragged up the Avenue to the circle.

The overland part of the operation was far more hectic. The sledge, all of wood, without any nails, was attached to a long rope, that should really have been made of hide. To the rope were attached a number of cross-bars to make hauling easier and increase the number of haulers on the rope. The hauling was done by the gallant Canford boys, who must have had one of the most strenuous mornings of their lives (Pl. 38).

We found that it took a minimum of thirty-two boys to move the sledge and stone, and that was only in fairly short bursts. To keep it going for longer spells and up slopes would have needed at least forty men, who would be presumed to be somewhat stronger than the boys.

Then we tried it with rollers under the sledge. This at once reduced the numbers by over half. Fourteen boys could now move it. What was difficult was handling the rollers and keeping the sledge on them. We had not got a large number and they were not very carefully shaped, so we found that getting a sufficient number into position between the heels of the last of the towing party and the front of the sledge, and keeping the sledge from sliding off at one side was not easy.

However, the experiment did show that bringing the bluestones from Pembrokeshire would not have been impossibly laborious, and would not have required very large numbers of people to do it, provided there was no great hurry.

What must have been a tremendous problem was bringing the sarsens from the Marlborough Downs, twenty miles away, where they occur naturally. A sledge large enough to take fifty tons is hard to conceive. Even using a large forked tree as a sledge, and young tree trunks as rollers, moving one of those must have taken several hundred men. Hauling a copy of one of those would indeed be an experiment.

The difficulties of this operation make the next stage described by Professor Piggott all the more remarkable, when some inspired architect decided banks and bluestones were far too trifling. Under his ambitious direction, the bluestones were removed, the problem of bringing the sarsens to the site solved, and the great stones of the outer ring and inner horseshoe set up.

Then came the two most problematical stages, when the fate of the displaced bluestones was decided. Round the sarsen outer circle are irregular rings of holes, known as the 'Z' and 'Y' holes. Their uncertain spacing seems to show that they could not be laid out from a central point, presumably because the sarsens got in the way. They may have been intended for the displaced bluestones but in fact they were never used. Mr Atkinson believes that twenty-two of the larger bluestones were dressed and put up in a setting in the centre, for which there is very little evidence except that it probably included two trilithons, as two lintels and various other signs of dressing can be seen to day. The 'Z' and 'Y' holes would have held the remaining sixty stones but some unknown event stopped this plan. Instead, the twenty-two dressed bluestones were taken down, the tenons battered off, and together with the other remaining bluestones they were put up in their present position in a circle inside the outer sarsens and in a horseshoe in the innermost position of all. You can see some of the evidence for this in a former bluestone lintel now in the circle, which has its mortices turned shamefacedly away from the sacred central area.

The dating of these last stages has been helped by Mr Atkinson's remarkable discovery of the now famous carvings on the stones. Late one summer day, when the sun low in the sky threw heavy shadows, he was photographing an inscription cut in one of the stones by some seventeenth-century vandal. Through the viewfinder of his camera he was astonished to see, below the inscription, a carving of a dagger and axehead on the surface of the stone, clearly outlined by the sun's shadows. It is extraordinary that these were never noticed before, but once they were, various others were soon found.

They are all weathered but the clearest ones show axe-blades and a hafted dagger. The bronze axe-blades are of a type known to have been in use in Britain between 1500 and 1000 B.C. They probably reflect the fact that the axe was a ceremonial symbol in many parts of the ancient world. It was the weapon of might and authority, in the same way as subsequently the double-headed axe formed part of the Etruscan fasces, as a sign of the king's power.

The dagger is thought by some people to be Mycenean. It is too worn for this ever to be certain, but if it is Mycenean, it confirms the date and circumstances in which the crowning stage of Stonehenge was reached.

Professor Piggott finally went on to explain how somewhere about 1500 B.C. the Beaker folk inhabitants of southern Britain suffered the same fate as they had dealt out to their predecessors, the Windmill Hill and Peterborough people. They were invaded by a warrior people from the continent, who have left traces of the wealth and glory of their warriors in the round disc and bell barrows in which they buried their dead.

Heavy stone maces, long narrow arrowheads with square-tipped barbs, bronze dagger blades with heavy ribs to reinforce them, and flanged axes reflect an advanced military and bronze-casting technique.

Gold, amber, faience and jet ornaments tell of both wealth and trading contacts with Ireland, the Baltic, Egypt and Greece. The gold cup found at Rillaton in Cornwall is very like one from a grave at Mycenae. A gold-encircled amber disc from the great palace at Knossos would not look at all out of place in a Wessex Bronze Age burial.

It is not surprising that this aristocracy, with its wealth, love of ostentation, command of technology, and connections with the Mediterranean should have produced someone with ideas as grandiose as those of the creator of the greatest stage of Stonehenge.

Whether the religion that was practised there had also made the long journey from Greece and Crete no authority can say. Stonehenge itself seems to have undergone the change which can be seen elsewhere from a monument primarily concerned with death and burial to a setting for some form of elaborate worship or ritual. The alignment shows that this was probably connected with the sun. With the growth of a richer and less self-contained society, the old utter dependence on the fertility of cattle and crops would have decreased. A more sophisticated form of religion may have been the result. But that is just speculation. What archaeologists do know is that the building of Stonehenge had nothing to do with the Druids, as is still believed by many people today. The Druids may have used Stonehenge as a place of worship just before the Roman invasion, but they certainly were not responsible for any surviving detail of it.

It is to the religious fervour of the Stone and Bronze Age inhabitants of Wessex that we must be grateful for this remarkable structure, which can still tell us much even if no one understands its exact purpose.

CHAPTER IX

THE ETRUSCANS

———

SOME SIXTY MILES north of Rome the town of Tarquinia stands on the brow of a small hill behind an untidy fringe of high, narrow, mediaeval towers. Between it and the sea lie the flat vegetable gardens of the Maremna, fields of artichokes split by the main coast road and railway north. Inland from the town a small road lined with dusty grey olive trees leads towards the distant mountains between cornfields that in April are a silky green as the wind and sun polish them. Scattered amongst these fields are a number of small triangular stone huts, fitted with heavy iron doors. Inside these a short flight of stairs takes you down to a series of small bright boxes cut in the soft, yellow stone. These boxes are usually square, about the size of a small room, and are decorated with some of the most famous relics of the Etruscans, their tomb paintings. The colours are bright and not those of nature. Blue birds sweep above pink dolphins, and the men are a dark red, in contrast to the pale women.

There is nothing mysterious about these paintings, like the remote strangeness of the Stone Age cave art. Their impact is on a lower level, but still a remarkable one. They convey simple pleasure. They are bright, decorative, pleasing, simple, and most of the time fairly easy to understand.

Many of them are fading or crumbling, but their unexpected unpretentious attraction has charmed many people into curiosity about their authors, the Etruscans. The Romans and Greeks become fixed in most people's minds by an imperceptible series of chance impressions, Ulysses and Horatius, pictures of the Acropolis and the Colosseum, Hollywood epics and visits to the Roman wall. Unless you are a specialist, the Etruscans are unlikely to be either hidden or half-illuminated by the debris of education. As one begins to learn about them, they become more intriguing. The Greeks and Romans gave them a bad reputation. They were immoral, pleasure-loving, degenerate, piratical, and borrowers of other people's art. D. H. Lawrence was a great admirer of them and saw in their passion for dancing and music a true expression of the spirit of

73

life. The Greeks were shocked by the way their women sat equally with the men at public occasions. Modern historians are hindered by the fact that Etruscan is one of the two major languages of the ancient world (the other is the language of the prehistoric civilization of the Indus valley) that has never been translated.

When Dr Daniel suggested they would make a good subject for 'Buried Treasure', I agreed at once. We were further encouraged by the magnificent Etruscan exhibition then at Zurich, which meant that much of the material needed for filming would be in one place.

In the event, the Zurich exhibition was so popular that Monday morning was the only time it was possible to get the camera and lights into the building without interfering with the public. We did a lot in the one morning we were there, but the rest of the programme, apart from a few shots in the British Museum, had to be taken during a glorious and hectic safari through Italy. I think I worked harder during that fortnight than ever before in my life. Cars breaking down, complications over permission to enter, permissions to film, liaison with the British Embassy and Italian television, arranging interpreters, and all the time the worry that we were overspending our already expensive budget were added to the actual labour of filming. Even with the gallant help of Dr and Mrs Daniel and an Italian electrician, the effort involved in lighting and filming six tombs in an afternoon, as we did at Tarquinia, has to be experienced to be believed.

Still, the sun shone on our picnics in the olive orchards, as we fortified ourselves with mortadella and bottles of Orvieto, the scenery was marvellous even if I never had time to see a single church or picture during our three days in Florence, and Dr Daniel invariably found the best place for us to eat in the evenings. The resulting programme was also the most satisfying to me from a selfish point of view of any in the series.

In the first place it relied least of all on personalities. No producer could have been more fortunate than I over the archaeologists who have made up the casts of 'Buried Treasure'. But even the most reliable personality cannot escape mood and circumstance, which does make for uncertainty on television, where spontaneity matters so much more than a script. With the best will in the world, my pre-occupation with the shape of the programme as a whole and putting it over to a mass audience did not always exactly match the archaeologist's scholarly attitude to the subject and concern that some implication might not get its proper treatment.

The Etruscan programme was almost entirely on film, which meant that every word and picture could be put in its exact place. Secondly there was so much material available to illustrate almost every part of Etruscan life that I had great scope for putting it together in a visually exciting way. And what glorious material it was. The problem was sorting it all out so that it would make sense.

From my reading on the subject I had first to evolve some kind of simplified history which we could then begin to illustrate with film. I started with the problem of the Etruscans' origin. The three possibilities are from the Alps, from the Eastern Mediterranean, or from some development or combination of local Italian peoples. The Alps theory was a nineteenth-century one that scarcely anyone accepts now. The oriental origins have the support of Herodotus, the Greek historian, who reported a legend that the Lydians, a people from Asia Minor, were driven by famine to take to their ships and eventually found their way to northwest and central Italy. Similarities between Etruscan and some of the early languages of Asia Minor, and in particular that of an inscription found on the Greek island of Lemnos support this, as does the strong oriental influence in early Etruscan art and life.

The supporters of the local Italian origin of the Etruscans say this eastern influence was a common phenomenon of the time, and merely reflects the spread of Greek and Syrian and Egyptian traders to the central Mediterranean. They have another Greek historian, the harmoniously named Dionysius of Halicarnassus, on their side, and are very strong amongst the present generation of Italian scholars. Many of these, though, are primarily experts in linguistics and the richly varied early languages of Italy. Archaeologists on the other hand see more significance in the sudden change from burning to burying their dead which marked the appearance of the Etruscans as a distinct people. This is more easily explained by invasion or occupation than sudden local development.

All that can be said for certain is that about the eighth century B.C. on the west coast of Italy there appear signs of a strongly developing civilization with a distinct character of its own. I decided it was impossible to go into these arguments in the programme. We simply had a map with moving arrows which showed the alternative theories.

Whether the Etruscans actually came from the East or only had contacts with it, they had all the impact of a city civilization on the Villanovans, a people living a Bronze Age life, not very different from that of the Bronze Age inhabitants of England.

Against the superior technology, weapons, and wealth of the Etruscans, they had little hope. Soon Etruscan cities were springing up in a half-circle north of Rome, between the Apennines and the sea. Many of them now lie under the foundations of modern cities, Perugia for instance,

Orvieto, on its extraordinary limestone plateau, and Chiusi, which was Clusium, the home of Lars Porsenna. Here again we had a map but we were able to add to it very decorative pictures of the cities themselves.

The ability to support the populations of these cities depended first on improved agriculture, and then on trade and skill in various crafts, particularly metal-working. Many of the fields and vineyards of modern Italy, like the cities, were first hacked out of the thick woods and barren scrub by the Etruscans. The method I used to illustrate this part of the programme required a considerable amount of organization. In the Etruscan exhibition was a little terracotta model of a plough with two oxen being driven by a farmer in a flat-brimmed conical hat. We filmed this on a turntable so that the model ploughman appeared to be making his furrow past the camera. Half-way past we then dissolved this shot to another of an actual modern plough with two oxen going on past the camera. We found the plough and oxen on the estate of our interpreter's father, who had a villa near Florence.

To match a painting of a long-horned, white bull at Tarquinia, we used even more abrupt methods. We simply drove up to a farm where I had seen some white cattle from the road, showed the farmer a copy of the painting, and asked him if we could film one of his cattle to match it. His reaction appeared to be that it would be in order for the British Broadcasting Corporation to arrive and film his cattle for a programme on the Etruscans any time they liked.

There can have been no lack of axes to cut down the forests or the Etruscans' Villanovan predecessors, where necessary, to provide fields for their ploughs. The Etruscans were some of the most skilled metal-smiths of the ancient world. The museums of Italy are full of their bronze vases, jugs, basins, and spiky candelabra-stands. Some of their decorative work is very beautiful too. A bronze mermaid about 8 inches long and a springing goat particularly caught my eye at the Zurich exhibition. They had a simplicity, an assurance, and a complete command of technique that was most pleasing. One particular type of bronze jug, sometimes copied as well in pottery, has been found in many places in north-west Europe. Like the white man's whisky amongst the North American Indians, the Etruscans' encouragement of a taste for wine amongst the Gauls must have considerably improved their export trade. But in the early stages their most important trading was done by sea. Much of their metal came from Sardinia and Elba, and the fleet which transported that could easily have gone further afield.

When we were filming, I was very anxious to find a representation of a ship to reflect this part of the Etruscan story. Various authorities described one on a grave-stone in the Bologna museum, but it turned out to be so worn that it would not have been visible on the screen. No one I asked could suggest another one. Then by great good luck I spotted one in the Royal Archaeological Museum in Florence. It was little larger than a stamp in size, on an ivory cup, which was itself a remarkable piece. The cup, which was of the seventh century B.C., and about 6 inches high, was covered with very battered bands of carving, which clearly showed in its decoration and representations of figures in kilts and long pigtails a strong Eastern influence. The ship had one crack right through the middle, but otherwise was beautifully clear. It had a single square sail, a sharply curved bow and stern, and, whether it was accurately observed or the carver's foible, the helmsman, contrary to the usual practice, held a large steering paddle over the port side. What was certainly copied from life was the large jar of wine which the helmsman had handy (Pl. 51).

From the numerous bays and harbours on the coasts of Etruria ships like these took the products of their metal workshops all round the Mediterranean, returning with minerals, Greek vases, and the luxuries, like ivory, of the East. In the course of doing this, historians report they also stole Hera's statue from the island of Samos, raped Bramon's wives in Attica, and sacked Athens. This did not make them very popular with the Greeks, who were their chief rivals anyway, and who took every opportunity to ruin their reputation by describing them as pirates.

It was in this period too, from the eighth to the seventh century B.C., that the Etruscan domination of Rome occurred. Rome was the most convenient ford over the Tiber on the way from Etruria to Campania, where there were numerous Etruscan colonies. Archaeology has confirmed the legends that the Etruscans took the obvious step in acquiring control of the ford. A vase was found on the Capitoline hill with Etruscan writing on it, and a tomb painting at Vulci with inscriptions refutes those who think the Etruscan origin of the Tarquins to be fiction.

The civilization that flourished on the proceeds of all this trade and military expansion was elaborate, cheerful, and luxurious. Fortunately for the programme, there is much visual evidence as to what it was like. There is a famous bucket, or *situla,* from Certosa, which is cast into bands of relief showing various scenes giving a good picture of Etruscan life about the sixth century B.C.

Round the top a military expedition sets off, first the cavalry, then the infantry, in three divisions, each with a differently shaped shield, and finally the lightly armed pioneers, each with an axe over his shoulder. In other bands, boars, deer, and hares are hunted, a ploughman drives home his two oxen, carrying his plough over his shoulder, and two men, attended by slaves, sit on a richly decorated couch playing the lyre and pan-pipes. But perhaps most typical of all is a funeral procession. This consists of numerous priests, slaves carrying offerings to accompany the dead man to the next world and firewood for the funeral pyre, an executioner carrying a great two-handed sword to sacrifice the ram which he is leading, and two slaves carrying, slung on poles, a bucket with the ashes of the dead man in it, exactly like the one on which these scenes are shown.

Funeral rites were responsible for two important parts of Etruscan life, their games and their tombs. The athletics, chariot-racing, and wrestling which marked the funeral of an important personage we filmed from many paintings and carvings. The wrestlers in the tomb of the Augurs at Tarquinia are one of the most remarkable paintings there. Two very powerful men, quite naked, with black side whiskers, grip each other's wrists in a tense paroxysm of muscular struggle (Pl. 48).

There is a painting of another sport at Tarquinia which does the Etruscans rather less credit. In this a man with a bag over his head wielding an unpleasant looking club is being gruesomely savaged by a dog, held on a long lead by another man. Whether it is right to condemn the Etruscans as a cruel people on the strength of this is doubtful, but there seems to be less doubt that the Roman's taste for gladiatorial combat grew out of such activities.

Their tombs frequently were designed as settings for life after death. In this way they reflect for us their everyday domestic life.

At Cerveteri, which was the Etruscan city of Caere, you cross the valley from the present town and come to the extraordinary necropolis, or city of the dead. This consists of a vast cluster of conical earth mounds, mostly in two long rows, making a sort of street. Some of them have been wired off and tidied up by the Italian government as a national monument. That sounds rather forbidding, but in fact it is a charming place. There are cypress trees and flowers higgledy-piggledy, and the tidying only goes as far as keeping the grass cut and removing litter. The tombs, which usually have a band of masonry round the base, and a single entrance, vary in size from about 20 feet across to a big one over a 100 feet in diameter (Pl. 45).

Inside, the soft rock is carved into chambers for the dead like the rooms they inhabited in life. There are couches, single and double beds with pillows accurately carved in stone, chairs like Victorian wickerwork ones only in stone, and little rooms leading off a central courtyard. One tomb has pillars and a sloping ceiling with beams, all imitated in rock from the real thing, and everywhere are painted carvings of domestic objects.

There are the lord's armour, weapons, and hunting dogs, and his lady's mirror in bronze surrounded by feathers to make it a fan also. Then there is a gambling board with a bag of counters, a pan which the guide swears is for making spaghetti, an attractive cat catching a lizard, and, my favourite, an unmistakable egg-whisk.

You can see what the exterior of their houses looked like from the Etruscan habit of making funerary urns to resemble them. There are any number of these in the museums, rectangular in shape, with sloping roofs and occasionally an elaborate ridge along the top.

Then at Marzabotto archaeologists have excavated the foundations of an Etruscan town that has not been built on subsequently. There you can see the little houses grouped in squares round a courtyard, all rigorously laid out north and south along the wide paved streets with a covered drain each side. Not only did the Romans inherit this type of town planning from the Etruscans, they also acquired much of their knowledge of architecture, including the arch, their skill in road and bridge making, irrigation, civil engineering, and sewerage. It is generally accepted now, for instance, that the Cloaca Maxima at Rome was Etruscan in origin.

The walls of great blocks of stone with which they surrounded their cities can still be seen at a number of places, like Perugia, Volterra, and Bolsena. With up to 100,000 inhabitants these cities must have been remarkable centres of civilization. The paintings reflect a cheerful life, in which banquets with much music and dancing played an important part (Pl. 41). Etruscan actors, jugglers, tumblers, and musicians all had a great reputation in the Roman world. The music of the lyre, double pipes, and long-curved trumpet seems to have accompanied most of their activities, from feasting to the punishment of slaves. The setting for these activities must have been attractive, too. The clothes they wore, as shown in the paintings, were brightly coloured and delicately worked, and were set off by their gold jewellery.

Etruscan jewellery is famous. Most of the great museums of Europe have collections of it. It is at once lavish, technically brilliant, and very modern in feeling. Much of it would not look the least out of place worn today. In fact, after I had shown the film we had taken of Etruscan jewellery to Prince Massimo, who is a well-known Etruscan collector, he pointed out to me the brooch his wife was wearing, a gold fish curved in a half circle. I had noticed how attractive it was, but never for a moment thought it might be 2,500 years old, until the Prince told me it was Etruscan.

Two techniques which they specialized in were making small animals like lions and winged horses, to decorate the elaborate fibulae, or safety pins, which were much worn, and the use of fine grains of gold to make patterns in relief. The secret of this technique was lost after the Etruscans and has only recently been re-discovered.

To see another surprising use to which they put gold, you have to delve as we did amongst the rather crowded cases of the archaeological museum at Florence. There you will find two human jaws which have a thin ribbon of gold carefully intertwined between the lower teeth. Skill in dentistry, you must admit, is a good index of civilization.

Like that of the Greeks and Romans the higher achievements of Etruscan civilization would have been impossible without a basis of slavery. At first Etruscan society was fairly simple. Each of the cities had a king, or *lucumo*, and the most important division beneath him was into families. There were no great social divisions within these families, and outside them, according to Pallottino, the only real lower class consisted of foreigners, acrobats, and servants.

In time the kings were replaced by a republican oligarchy, a ruling body of nobles, who were at once judges, priests, and military leaders. From the kings, the republican magistrates inherited their symbols of authority, the golden crowns, the sceptre, the purple robe, the throne, and the ill-fated fasces, made up of the ceremonial axe of the king and the wooden rods for corporal punishment ordered by him as magistrate. The Etruscans in turn passed these on to the Romans, and so they reached us.

The ruling families eventually became so much an upper class—for instance, marriage was forbidden with the lower classes—that there were a number of rebellions against their rule, but the importance of the family to them is interesting to us for another reason. They were the first European people to use what we call a Christian name and surname. It was Lars Porsenna, not Lars son of Larth, as it would have been in the East.

I have already said that these ruling families produced priests as well as magistrates and generals. This was a result of the nature of their religion, which consisted largely of reading and interpreting the divine will. Groups of them are shown in various engravings clustered round the still smoking liver of a newly sacrificed animal. Others specialized in interpreting thunderbolts, of which the nine great gods controlled one, Jupiter alone wielding three, or studied the flights of birds. By these means minute and complicated instructions were given for laying the foundations of cities, building temples, surveying land, and for making decisions in war and peace. As well, prophetic books dealt with the destinies of men and life after death.

That so much is known of the Etruscan religion is in part due to the most curious of all their relics, a bronze model of a sheep's liver. This is

41 & 42. ABOVE. A banqueting scene. An Etruscan painting from the Tomb of the Leopards at Tarquinia. BELOW. An Etruscan painting from the Tomb of Hunting and Fishing at Tarquinia.

43 & 44. ABOVE. Filming a long-horned cow in central Italy identical with one shown in one of the Etruscan painted tombs at Tarquinia. BELOW. Picknicking on the summit of the hill on which Montefiascone stands during the filming for the 'Buried Treasure' programme on the Etruscans.

45 & 46. ABOVE. Etruscan tomb in the City of the Dead at Caere. BELOW. The Porta Marzia at Perugia. Though added to by the Romans the arch is probably Etruscan.

47 & 48. Etruscan paintings from the Tomb of the Augurs at Tarquinia. ABOVE. A double-pipe player. BELOW. Wrestlers.

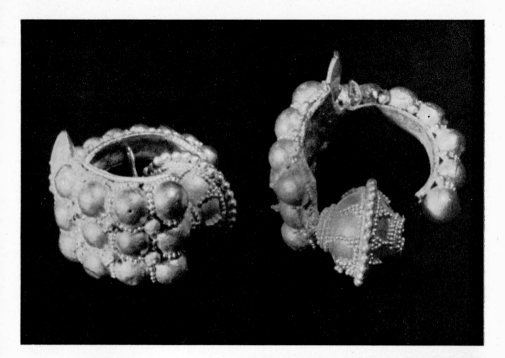

49 & 50. ABOVE. A pair of Etruscan gold ear-rings enlarged to about four times actual size. BELOW. The chimaera. A magnificent example of Etruscan metal-working in the Royal Archaeological Museum, Florence.

51 & 52. ABOVE. An Etruscan ship. Detail from a seventh-century B.C. ivory cup. BELOW. Etruscan nobleman playing the pan pipes. Detail from the bronze *situla* or bucket of Certosa.

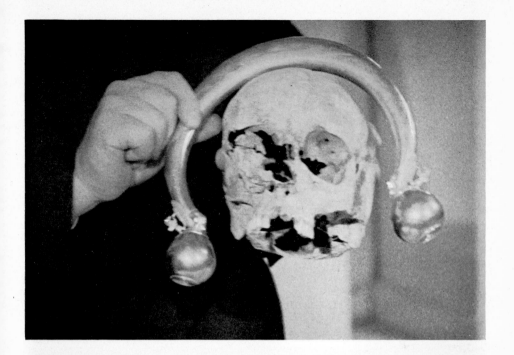

53 & 54 ABOVE. The gold headband of Vix round the skull of the Celtic princess with which it was buried. BELOW. Detail of the filigree work on the base of the 2,500-year-old headband of Vix.

55 & 56. ABOVE. Winged horse, whose long hair possibly shows its Scythian origin, on the base of the gold headband of the Princess of Vix. BELOW. Glyn Daniel and M. René Joffroy standing by the great bronze vase of Vix.

57 & 58. ABOVE. Group of horses' heads from one of the chariot groups round the neck of the Vix vase. BELOW. The gorgon's face on the handle of the great bronze vase of Vix.

59 & 60. ABOVE. The great ditches and ramparts which form the southern defences of Maiden Castle. BELOW. Maiden Castle from the air.

61 & 62. ABOVE. Bombarding the western defences of Maiden Castle with arrows from a working copy of a Roman Legion's catapult. BELOW. A coastal hill-fort in Brittany similar to those in which the Veneti safeguarded their women and children while they were at sea. They probably introduced multiple defence ditches to Maiden Castle when they were driven out of Brittany by Julius Caesar.

63. Arrowhead in the spine of a defender of Maiden Castle, as revealed by excavation. This is now on show in the Dorchester Museum.

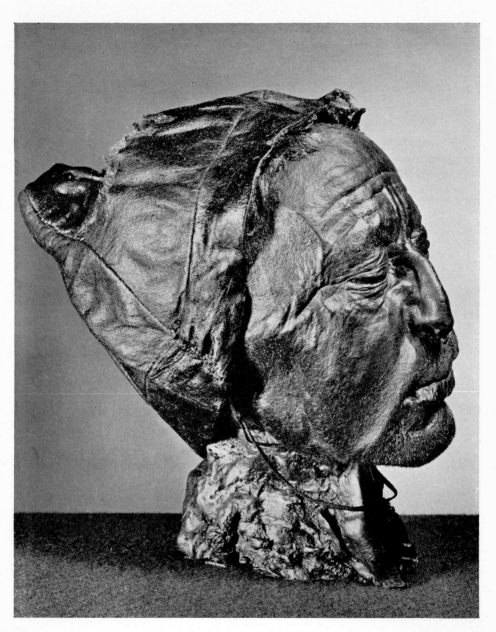

64. The 2,000-year-old head of Tollund Man.

65. A victim being sacrificed to the gods, as Tollund Man may have been. Detail from the Gundestrup Bowl in the National Museum, Copenhagen.

66. The 2,000-year-old body of Tollund Man just after it had been removed from the peat bog where it was found.

67. Noëlle Middleton cooking an Iron Age meal in a television studio. In the saucers are samples of the seeds that were found in Tollund Man's stomach.

covered with the names of the gods who controlled various parts of the heavens, and was a guide to the haruspex, the interpreter of the sacrifice. With it we made an effective film sequence for the programme. There is an engraving on a bronze mirror showing a haruspex bending over a liver which had just been extracted from a sacrifice. From a close-up of the liver in the engraving, we went to a close-up of the model liver, an almost exact match.

The absolute acceptance of the gods' ruling on so many activities must have been an inhibiting form of fatalism. Perhaps, when all was going well, their cheerful approach to life was encouraged by not having to work out any vital decisions: eat, drink, and be merry for tomorrow the sacrificial liver decides whether the army retreats or advances. If we could understand Etruscan, we might know more about the effect of this attitude on Etruscan fortunes in the fifth century B.C.

About sixty or seventy words can be translated with confidence, mostly from inscriptions on tombs. Many methods have been tried but the world still awaits a new Champollion, someone who will elucidate another Rosetta stone with a Latin and Etruscan version of the same passage long enough to solve the problem. Then historians will be able to read the linen book, cut into strips and used to wrap the mummy of an Egyptian woman in Roman times, which at the moment is the longest piece of Etruscan known.

In moments of national danger, their fatalism was matched by the reluctance of the twelve great cities, who made up the Etruscan league, to come to each other's help. The great noble families who had escaped from the rule of their kings, and were jealous of any individual gaining too much power, seemed decidedly opposed to any suggestion of submitting to a common leader, and fatalism further discouraged any political expediency which might have demanded it.

The result was that their power which looked at one time as though it might unite the whole of Italy was reduced piecemeal. The Gauls swept down from the Alps, sacking their cities in the north. The Latins attacked their south-eastern territories. The Greek cities in the south of Italy defeated their fleet in a great sea-battle off Cumae, and ravaged their undefended sea coast.

But most dangerous of all was the growing power of Rome. Off and on for a hundred years Rome and the neighbouring city of Veii fought each other. Finally, in 396 B.C., after a ten-year siege, Veii fell. During all that time not one of the other Etruscan cities came to her help. This part of the story I illustrated simply with a shot of the ruins of Veii. It was ample comment on the penalty of disunion.

F

As a military and naval power, the Etruscans' day was over. An epidemic of malaria had a similar effect on their economic strength. Only in the arts was there any sign of revival.

The status of Etruscan art is a questionable matter. Many authorities consider it to be poorly derived from Greek art, and its native characteristics to be rustic and crude. But recently there has been a revival of interest in it. Certainly much jewellery, metalwork, and the early black pottery have great elegance and simplicity. The painting and sculpture, too, often has a realism, individuality, and richness of character that contributed greatly to Roman art and even possibly to the great Tuscan painters of the Renaissance.

In its first phase, from the eighth to the fifth century B.C., the main influence on their art as a whole was Eastern. In the second place, it was Greek.

Though their habits declined into an increasing concern for pleasure and luxury, and their religion which once had inspired the cheerful tomb-painting of Tarquinia became more and more obsessed with the horrors of life after death, this Greek influence did produce some famous works. There is the Apollo of Veii and many smaller pieces in the Villa Giulia museum in Rome, and you can see two particularly well-known examples in a gallery of the archaeological museum in Florence, the more than life-size bronze figure of the orator, and the Chimaera (Pl. 50). This is a lion with a serpent for a tail, which is biting the horn of a goat's head that grows out of the lion's back. This extraordinary piece is a magnificent example of metal-work but it is a macabre conception, to say the least. There is a story that it was discovered in the Middle Ages by some peasants who promptly buried it again in horror at finding such a monster. It shares something of the feeling which produced the painting of the demon Tuculcha in one of the later tombs. He has the face of a vulture, the ears of a donkey, is armed with serpents, and implacably herds rich and poor alike to their mournful fate in the afterworld.

But neither an artistic revival nor religious doubts could stop the growing power of Rome. By battle, siege, alliance, or occupation, the Etruscan cities fell piecemeal. By the time of Hannibal's invasion, they were an unimportant military asset to either side. By the middle of the first century B.C. they had ceased to have any independent existence as a people. Like the ruins of Veii, a film shot which we showed of the barren plateau where Tarquinia once stood underlined the fate of the city which might have been to the world what Rome became.

This story had all the dramatic shape one could wish for. My only worry was whether the filmed material to illustrate it would become static and monotonous. I think the result managed to avoid this simply because there were so many elements to it. Paintings, sculpture, scenery, jewellery, architecture, animated maps, and metal-work really did seem to give enough scope to keep the watching eye lively and interested. I rounded the programme off with a sequence which showed an imaginary day in the life of an Etruscan noblewoman. This had no academic basis whatsoever as the material came from all sorts of periods and places, but it seemed to make good television. With scenes from paintings, carvings and vases, I showed the heroine doing her make-up in the morning, choosing her clothes and jewellery, studying the contents of the kitchen larder, attending some funeral games with her husband and so on, while the children went swimming or fishing in the lake, and the eldest son tried on his new suit of armour. The climax was the banquet and dance in the evening.

There are any number of dancers shown in the Etruscan tomb paintings, as well as musicians playing the harp and double pipe. I had a short piece of music specially composed for harp and flute in an imaginary Etruscan idiom, with a strong dance rhythm. We then edited the pictures of the dancers so they changed on the beat of the music. The result probably bore no relation to the reality 2,500 years ago, but you did get from it an odd feeling of something very remote but convincing.

As a subject, the Etruscans were interesting, strange, and in many ways attractive, and I think we were right to include them in the series, apart from their television possibilities, because after all they were responsible for passing on to the Romans, and so ultimately to us, much of the heritage of Greece, as well as the achievements of their own particular genius.

CHAPTER X

THE PROUD PRINCESS

———

CHÂTILLON SUR SEINE is a quiet country town in eastern France. It lies some way north of the famous Burgundy vineyards near Dijon, and although the wheatfields and wooded valleys of the upper reaches of the Seine are an attractive change from the monotonous beet fields of the Pas de Calais, few English people bother to stop there on their way to the Riviera.

For many years philosophy and history were taught at the local Lycée at Châtillon by Monsieur René Joffroy. It would be no insult to Monsieur Joffroy to say that he appears unmistakably French. He is short and stocky, is unrestrained in gesture, and when you meet him setting off purposefully to pursue his hobby in a tartan shirt and corduroy riding breeches, his neatly circular bald patch uncovered by a hat faintly recalls a tonsure. His hobby, which has kept him happy and busy for many years, is well suited to an inhabitant of Châtillon, which lies on one of the main ancient trade routes between Italy and Switzerland and northern France and England. The Iron Age Celts, the Gauls, and then the Romans all appreciated the strategic nature of Mont Lassois, an abrupt, flat-topped hill half a mile long and a quarter wide, which both dominates the valley of the Seine and has a spring on the top. In the late nineteenth century a large iron bowl mounted on a tripod and surmounted with griffons' heads gave the locality the credit for having produced one of the better known masterpieces of Iron Age metal-work. So there was plenty of scope for an archaeologist.

Local pottery from 600 B.C. to Roman times in its varying types, beads, buckles, and weapons were uncovered and classified in large quantities. Excavations revealed the foundations of huts on the top of the Mont and the Roman fortifications that overlaid the cruder ones of the Gauls. Studying all this was a busy, if unspectacular, occupation, but all the time Monsieur Joffroy had at the back of his mind the possibility of discovering the burial place of the people of the Mont. After six years of work the clue to this at last came from his right hand man and helper, Jean Moisson.

84

Moisson is a peasant small-holder and the grave-digger of Vix, the small village at the foot of the Mont. A man of great courtesy and dignity, he is also shrewd beneath the apparent slowness of his manner, and instantly observant of any peculiarity in the local landscape. He had noticed that a farmer ploughing the field next to his, just below the Mont, had uncovered some alien stones. They were good stones, suitable for building, unlike the soft local ones, and must have been brought from a quarry some way away for a purpose.

However, they were so thinly laid and meagre that Monsieur Joffroy, hastily summoned on his motor bicycle, decided they were probably just the foundation of a Gaulish house. The correctness of his decision to investigate nevertheless was proved when their digging and clearing revealed that in fact this was a destroyed burial mound.

The stones that had once helped to make it 40 yards in diameter and 20 feet high had been used by the Gauls in the Roman period to pave a nearby road, where the remains of the stones could still be seen.

The excitement and size of the band of helpers grew. But all in vain. After two days nothing had appeared except water which poured into the excavation. Discouraged, Joffroy went home. Moisson, whose home in the village of Vix is only a few hundred yards away, stayed on to clear up. Idly he turned over a stone, and there was something that most definitely was not just another rock stuck in the chilly February mud.

Monsieur Joffroy's Sunday peace was disturbed very urgently and early the following morning. Moisson thought that what he had seen was part of a metal saddle. Excited digging soon disproved that. It was in fact the handle of a gigantic bronze vase. This time a pump was brought to keep the water back and eventually the vase was got out. It was somewhat battered and crushed and the base was broken off, but even so it was quite remarkable. Restored, it stands nearly 5 feet high and weighs about a quarter of a ton.

Two days later Joffroy went back and discovered that he had come on a burial chamber about 12 feet square that had been lined and covered with wood. With the decay of the wood, the stones on top had fallen in and badly crushed the contents. On the other hand, the removal of the mound to pave the road meant there had been nothing to attract the attention of subsequent grave robbers.

Along one side of the chamber were laid four iron wheels. They explained the nature of the burial. The body had been laid on the floor of a chariot surrounded by gifts and offerings for the journey into the next world. Of the skeleton, only the head had survived the fall of the roof. It belonged to a woman of about 30 to 35 years of age. Just behind where it had fallen off lay perhaps the greatest treasure of all, a gold headband. This was semi-circular in shape, rounded, and about half an inch in diameter with, at each end, a lion's paw gripping a globe a little smaller than a golf ball. This headband went over the top of the head, not round it, with the globes coming in front of the ears. The bottoms of the globes are decorated with amazingly delicate concentric rings of gold filigree work, while on the top of them, standing on the outside of the headband itself, are two little winged horses. The workmanship of these is again incredible. They are no larger than the nail of a little finger, yet even the hairs of the horses' coats and the lions' claws have been lightly sketched in with the utmost precision (Pls. 54 & 55).

No comparable piece to this has ever been found, so it is literally priceless. Nor has its 2,500 years of existence done it any damage. From its flawless sheen it might have come straight out of a Bond Street jewellers. Its origin is uncertain but some experts think it may come from Scythia, north of the Black Sea, because of the long-haired coats of the winged horses, which are typical of that region.

Besides this, the other pieces of the jewellery look more like the play-things of a country child, but in all her finery the princess of Vix must have been a spectacular sight. Round each ankle she had a hollow bracelet of bronze, while round her neck went a thin, solid bronze ring, which had once been bound round with leather in a spiral pattern.

Seven fibulas, or decorated safety-pins, had fastened her clothes. These were of worked iron or bronze, and four of the bronze ones were decorated with a flat disc of red amber mounted above a stud of coral.

Round each wrist she wore three bracelets of polished schist and a fourth of amber beads threaded on a fine bronze ribbon. Finally, to complete the ensemble, there was a necklace of three larger amber beads, four smaller ones, and four rings of polished black and white stone.

Next to the gold headband, the most remarkable of the other objects in the grave was the great bronze vase. With its height of 5 feet, and its quarter-of-a-ton weight, it is the largest single metal object that survives from antiquity. The body of the vase, which would hold about 1,100 litres, is hammered out of a single sheet of bronze. That its makers had the skill to produce a single sheet as large as this is alone remarkable. It has two large handles, decorated with beautifully worked serpents' heads and the face of a gorgon, carried out with great realistic effect and detail, down to the row of curls on the forehead and the overlapping eye-teeth (Pl. 58).

Round the neck of the vase runs a frieze of figures in relief, eight chariots drawn by four horses each, with a driver and a hoplite, an armed Greek infantry soldier, between each. The drivers, dressed in helmet and tunic, each hold reins made of a thin ribbon of metal leading to the groups of horses, each one of which is different. The soldiers wear a cuirass, leg-armour, and a helmet with a large crest.

With its simplicity, strength, and detail this relief is a masterpiece.

Where the vase came from is a problem. The style of the decoration is unmistakably Greek. On the other hand there is a different answer in the letter which each group of horses had on its back to correspond with one on the neck of the vase, so that they could be put in the correct position. The craftsman who had marked them this way used Etruscan letters. Perhaps the body of the vase was made in Etruria by their skilled bronze-smiths and decorated with a frieze brought from Greece or a Greek colony in Italy. In any case, bringing it to Burgundy, either by mule-back or in a rough cart, must have been an immense labour.

There was also a cover with two handles for the vase. This was pierced by a pattern of small holes in a petal shape, presumably for draining the wine, and in the centre was a small hub with a flattened top. On this stood a bronze statuette of a hooded woman, about 6 inches high, of a beautifully simple style.

There had also been placed on the cover two small Greek pottery vases, and a small silver bowl with a plain gold globe in its centre. This silver bowl showed signs of having been wrapped in a cloth before it was placed in the tomb, for some traces of vegetable fibre were still found attached to it. One of the Greek vases, a flat, two-handled type called a Droop cup after the well-known classical scholar, had a band underneath it decorated in red and black with a scene of Greek soldiers fighting Amazons. The other vase was plain black.

At the foot of the vase was a bronze jug, whose clover-leaf-shaped rim and handle ending in a palm leaf marked it clearly as Etruscan. There were also in the tomb two plain bronze bowls and a great, flat, bronze basin, which was probably used for some form of ceremonial cleansing.

Of the body of the chariot, little was found except a number of bronze plaques, rather like horse brasses. The four wheels, which were laid along one side of the grave, were about $2\frac{1}{2}$ feet in diameter and were shod with iron. Each had eight spokes and they fitted into beautifully worked and impressive bronze hubs.

The dating of this find is reasonably exact. The Droop cup was made in Athens between 530-520 B.C. Judging by similar ones of a smaller size that have been found elsewhere, the bronze vase must also date from the second half of the sixth century B.C. The local jewellery is typical of this period too, as is the Etruscan jug. In fact, everything agrees in a convincing way that the date was just before 500 B.C.

What is not so clear is how and why this treasure got to Vix. The conventional answer is trade. There is no doubt that Mont Lassois was in a commanding position to take tolls from the tin of Cornwall and the amber of the Baltic, as it met the metal-work, pottery, wines, and jewellery of Greece and Etruria going the other way. Oddly enough, the latter did not arrive via the Rhône valley, the obvious geographical route. Some aggressive tribe must have blocked that way because there are no signs there of the movement of traders. On the other hand they can be traced from find to find through Switzerland. So the great bronze vase must have come to Vix the hard way over the Alps.

But I find it difficult to account for the Princess entirely in terms of customs dues. Are we to suppose that every ruler of the Mont was buried in such state, and all their graves wait to be found, or have been despoiled without leaving a trace? Or alternatively was there just one moment when trade was so flourishing that they could afford such a rich burial? Even so, wouldn't it be a little odd to bury such an exceptional object as the vase with a young woman, unless there was a special reason?

No, I think a clue to it can be found in the 'Histories' of Herodotus, the fifth-century B.C. Greek historian. On page 40 of Aubrey de Selincourt's translation in the Penguin Classics you can read about a 'bronze bowl large enough to hold two thousand five hundred gallons and covered with small figures round the outside of the rim.' It is a pity Herodotus does not say more, because so far the description would fit the Vix vase exactly.

Herodotus' bowl was made by the Lacedaemonians, the inhabitants of Sparta, to give to Croesus, the notoriously rich king of Lydia, who had befriended them. In fact, Croesus never got this great bronze gift. The Lacedaemonians said the islanders of Samos captured it on its way to Croesus, but the Samians said the Lacedaemonians sold it to them when they heard Croesus had been defeated and made prisoner. Either way, it ended up as an offering in the Temple of Hera, the wife of Zeus and the goddess of marriage, on Samos.

Herodotus frequently also describes the gifts that were made to oracles, like the famous one at Delphi. We know a great bronze bowl like the Vix one was given as an offering at about this period and that oracles were always being given gifts. I think then that the Princess of Vix may have been a famous local oracle, that the basin and small vases were part of her professional equipment, and that the great vase and gold diadem were gifts for successful advice or prophecy.

Be that as it may, the Vix treasure is a most marvellous find. As well as showing the impact of civilization on the rough Celtic warriors whose invasions were a constant trouble to Britain in the five hundred years before the Romans, the find also gives remarkable evidence of the ramifications of Etruscan trade, and the vase and headband are of outstanding interest.

As a subject, it made one of the most complete and satisfying 'Buried Treasure' programmes. There was not too much complicated material, there was a good human story to it, and the objects with so much fine detail filmed superbly. If one longed to have been there with a film camera when the find was made, there were at least still photographs of the various stages of the discovery, and we shot Joffroy and Moisson pointing out the details of the actual sites. From them, too, we heard all the information at first hand which has been included here. Altogether it was one of the pleasantest of all the programmes to do.

It is pleasing, too, to think of Monsieur Joffroy, busy with his research as well as being curator of a thriving local museum where the treasure is kept, and happily taking advantage in his travels of the considerable international reputation as an archaeologist which the 'chariot burial of Vix' has given him.

CHAPTER XI

MAIDEN CASTLE

A MILE OR TWO to the south of the Roman walls of Dorchester, just off the Weymouth road, lies a long, low hill. Anybody seeing it for the first time is almost certain to look twice, for the bare hump of its crest is coiled round and round with enormous ditches and banks. This is Maiden Castle, but no ivy-held masonry or crumbling Gothic towers justify such a name. Its ramparts are entirely earthen. It is an Iron Age hill fort, not the largest in the country as the notices carefully say, but undoubtedly the finest.

If you want to impress an American visitor, here is the answer. The casual air which the short grass and the cows cropping give it makes the truly vast extent of the ditches and banks all the more striking. But then it begins to disappoint a little. It is so empty. Except in an aerial photograph, it is difficult to take in its defences as a whole. You can try to imagine what impulse drove men to all that labour, and whether they were pleased when they had finished, but there does not seem to be any obvious answer, and soon the sun on the distant cliffs of the Isle of Wight becomes more attractive than wondering about the Iron Age.

Yet in fact a visit to the Dorchester Museum will soon show you that this is one of the best understood of all the great ancient monuments of these islands. This is because it was the scene of a classic series of excavations by Sir Mortimer Wheeler between 1934 and 1938.

Beneath that featureless turf were found an elaborate but comprehensible mingling of earth layers and remains which told a remarkable story. Unlike the other great prehistoric monuments I have talked about so far, Maiden Castle is not the result of a religious impulse. Its cause lay in war, or the threat of war. But its history as Sir Mortimer describes it starts a long time before fear raised those elaborate defences.

Some time before the West Kennet long barrow was built, man left the first traces on the easternmost of the two knolls which crown the hill we now know as Maiden Castle. These consisted of two ditches, 8 to 12 feet broad and 5 feet deep, with a number of causeways crossing them, encircling about 10 acres. No hut sites, however, were found within them.

If Professor Piggott's interpretation of the causewayed camp of Windmill Hill is correct, this is not surprising. In his report on the excavation, Sir Mortimer refers to the 'causeways or interruptions normal to neolithic ditches of the "Windmill Hill" series'. The cooking pits and the sherds of round-bottomed, bag-shaped pottery which the excavators found here probably belonged to the camps of herders making the regular round-up of straying cattle.

Just as the Windmill Hill people were succeeded by others who treated their dead in a more sophisticated way, so at Maiden Castle the next stage Sir Mortimer traced reflects an extraordinary burial. A dark turf line seems to show that the original camp, after a lengthy occupation, was abandoned and became grown over. Then the site which had once been chosen as a commanding one for gathering in cattle was marked by a great burial mound, 5 feet or more high with a 12-foot broad ditch on each side, which stretched for the extraordinary length along the ridge of 1,790 feet, over four times the length of the West Kennet long barrow. Near the eastern end of this mound was found a body in a sufficiently unusual state to match the mound which marked its last resting place.

Shortly after death the victim's limbs had been hacked from his body, and his skull had been operated on, apparently to get at his brain. You can see this macabre relic in Dorchester Museum today. The bones show clearly the hacked marks from stray blows near the breaks, and you can ponder on just how, with a flint knife, the neat roundel was hacked, sawn or scraped out of the skull, before a more brutal assault on the base finally collapsed the whole brain-case and gave the desired access to the brain.

Why this was done is as mysterious as most manifestations of neolithic religion. Ceremonial cannibalism, to acquire the strength of the dead, has been practised from the time of Pekin man to New Guinea today. Sir Mortimer believes this may be another example of it.

Certainly the existence of the long mound once again attracted people to the site. The ditches on each side were convenient shelter for camp fires, and amongst the ashes were found sherds of pottery which told the same story of the succession of peoples as at West Kennet, Windmill Hill— Peterborough—Beaker.

But after that comes what Sir Mortimer calls the 'Bronze Age hiatus'. The successive cultures of Food Vessel and the Urn people kept mostly to the valleys. Travel and an occasional burial mound alone disturbed the downland. The single Bronze Age spearhead there Sir Mortimer has evocatively likened to a cartridge case dropped by some solitary hunter in his chase through the hilly scrub.

Through the subsequent invasions, and the Deverel-Rimbury and Hallstatt cultures, Maiden Castle still remained unoccupied. It was not until 300 B.C. or so that famine intensified invasion from the continent and led to activities not unlike those of 1940. Hastily-dug ditches and banks appeared on suitable hill-tops to leave a memory of our prehistoric ancestors as familiar as the long and round barrows.

The wetter weather also made the downland once more as suitable as the valley for settlements. So in the circumstances, the hill was again lived on about 250 B.C.

Unlike earlier Iron Age hill forts, which were simply defended enclosures used in moments of danger but not normally occupied, Maiden Castle's defences sheltered a permanent settlement. Sir Mortimer's report describes traces of a road, rectangular huts, food storage pits, and even remains of a bun or loaf, that had been over-baked and so had survived. These occupied about 16 acres of the eastern knoll, and were protected by a rampart, 12 feet high and wide, with timber facings, and outside that a ditch, 50 feet wide and 20 deep. In the next stage, the whole of the hill-top, some 45 acres, was enclosed. The rampart and ditch used for this were of a different type. The rampart had no upright face. Instead its slope was an extension of that of the ditch, making a steep continuous climb at the top of which any attacker would arrive breathless. Where it joins the first rampart there is no sudden break. What had happened was that the timber facing had decayed and allowed the first rampart to tumble and spread, making in fact a continuous slope with the ditch.

At about the same time as the extension of the fort to cover the whole hill-side there was another important event. The eastern entrance was remodelled and given the extra protection of a barbican, or outwork. But if this took place, as Sir Mortimer estimates, about 200 B.C., a much greater elaboration happened some 150 years later. Then the principle of outer defences, which were already expressed in the barbicans guarding the entrances, was applied to the whole camp. The main rampart was much enlarged and given the additional protection of two outer ramparts on the south side, and one on the more easily defended north side.

Now the story of Maiden Castle so far, though interesting enough, was not particularly suitable for television. No method could quite reproduce on the small screen the sense of vastness and applied effort which walking round its defences gives one. We filmed the site itself and the neolithic skeleton, with its strangely hacked limbs and skull, in Dorchester Museum. We had models made which showed very effectively the different stages through which the great fort reached its present appearance. But I didn't think there was anything here yet which would hold a mass audience to archaeology against the capering comics of the rival wavelength.

Where I did see a promising story was in the fascinating detective methods of Sir Mortimer in working out the origins of the change of methods in the defences, and in his dramatic account of the final capture of Maiden Castle by the Romans.

The sudden multiplication of the defences must have had a reason, and he found it in the sling and the necessity for improved defences to keep slingers at bay. That raised the problem of who wielded this new weapon which so altered the appearance of Maiden Castle, and where did they come from. This in turn set off a long process of search and elimination which eventually led him to Brittany. But first, I had to find a slinger. This was much easier than I expected. The curator of Chester Museum, whom I asked because of the Museum's association with Roman warfare, knew an ex-Cambridge undergraduate who had made a hobby of slinging. His performance at Maiden Castle, which we filmed, completely changed my ideas of the weapon with which David slew Goliath. I had no idea a stone could be propelled so simply with such power and accuracy.

A sling consists of a small piece of leather with two long strings joined to it on each side. A smooth pebble about the size of a small hen's egg is placed in the piece of leather, the sling is then whirled round the head until one string is let go, when the stone whizzes off for more than a hundred yards. It never ceased to astonish me that the stone always came out in the right direction, but it did, and if you stood in front of the slinger the hum as it rushed overhead sounded almost like a bullet.

Having seen a slinger in action, I quite understood why the defenders of Maiden Castle raised those great ditches and banks. As well as protecting the inhabitants, the ramparts would tire any attackers, making them an easier target for defending slingers, who would have the commanding advantage of height, an important factor in sling warfare.

Then in the excavations great hoards of sling-stones were found, dumps of ammunition brought from Chesil Beach half a dozen miles away.

The origin of the people who used them next took us to Brittany, where the local paper produced surely one of the most unusual headlines ever inspired by television. 'La BBC television anglaise filme les oppidums gauloises de Finistere.' Still, these oppidums gauloises, or cliff castles as we called them, were a vital link in the chain, as well as being spectacular enough to please any film producer.

In the thirties, Sir Mortimer and his helpers scoured northern and western France looking for parallels with the sling-stone defences of Maiden Castle. Only in the cliff castles of Brittany did they find any (Pl. 62).

The cliff castles were small rocky promontories jutting out into the sea, where the Veneti, the local tribe of Gauls, safeguarded their families when they were away at sea fighting or trading for tin in Cornwall. They were protected by the cliffs and waves to seaward, and by ditches and banks across the neck of the promontories to landward. They were very picturesque sites, standing stark and rugged against the sea, miles from anywhere, only reached either by farm tracks at the best or on foot. Little hollows in the more sheltered slopes show where the huts of turf and branches stood. It must have been a bleak existence, waiting there for the fleet's return, guarded by a few slingers and the ramparts. Though the defences are slight compared with Maiden Castle, the evidence for their association with sling-warfare is clear. There were plenty of stones on the beaches close at hand and many have been found on the site themselves.

Furthermore, there is an historical event which fits in with this evidence. In 56 B.C. Julius Caesar decided to teach a thorough lesson to this most difficult and rebellious tribe of Gauls. He defeated their fleet in a great sea-battle probably somewhere in Quiberon Bay, put all their senate to death, and sold into slavery any of the rest of the tribe whom he could seize.

Cornwall, which they knew from their trading, would be the obvious refuge for those of the Veneti who could escape. It is also likely that it was the men, with their knowledge of slings and ramparts, rather than the women with their skill at pottery, who succeeded in getting there.

In Cornwall there are numerous cliff castles, like Trevelgue, near Newquay, which bear a strong resemblance to those in Brittany. At Bulbury Camp, between Poole and Maiden Castle, there has been found an Iron Age anchor which seems clearly Venetic in origin. It was attached by chain rather than rope, a point specially noted by Caesar in his comparison between the ships of the Romans and the Veneti.

Sir Mortimer's theory then, which I tried to turn into television, is that in the middle of the first century B.C., a largely male handful of the Veneti were driven out of Brittany by Julius Caesar and escaped to the west of England. Here they imposed their rule and their ideas of warfare on the unenterprising local inhabitants. The comparative fewness of the refugees, determined though they were, and in particular the scarcity of women (the potters of the time), may explain why the sudden change in the defences of Maiden Castle was accompanied only by a partial change of the local pottery styles.

You may argue that the ditches and banks of the Brittany cliff castles bear little resemblance in size to those of Maiden Castle. But the outline of Maiden Castle already existed with a single ditch and guarded entrances in the first century B.C. It was the requirements of sling-stone warfare applied to an already large town, rather than a little rocky promontory, which produced the great ramparts we know today.

Maiden Castle had two more important changes before the defences were put to their final test. At about the turn of the century the defences reached the final stage of elaboration in which we see them today, weathered by age. As Sir Mortimer says, 'This phase represents the work of a master-mind, wielding unquestioned authority and controlling vast resources of labour. The whole plan is now knit together into a single unit, with a single personality.'

Some twenty to thirty years later, about A.D. 25, the command of the great fortress changed hands again. During the troubled reign of King Cunobelin, Shakespeare's Cymbeline, the Belgae, who had been in occupation of south-eastern England for some time, brought new pottery, new habits, and a new discipline to Maiden Castle. The defences were repaired and refaced, and it was no tumbling ruin which the second Augustan Legion under the command of the future Roman Emperor Vespasian had to besiege in A.D. 44.

When I was preparing the programme on Maiden Castle an enterprising journalist rang me up and asked if I was organizing a battle between Romans and ancient Britons. Unfortunately I had to say no. 'Buried Treasure' has to make do without the resources of Hollywood. But at the cost of a few pounds and with the ingenuity of E. W. Marsden, lecturer in Ancient History at Liverpool University, we were able to show viewers a working copy of a Roman legion's light artillery in action, in contrast to the slings of the defending Britons (Pl. 61).

Mr Marsden has made a special study of ancient siege artillery and seemed very pleased to make a working copy of a catapult and bring it to Maiden Castle for us to film it in action. Before I met him, my idea of a catapult was a machine with a long arm which hurled stones or dead horses into besieged towns. In fact a Roman legion's catapult, or lesser scorpion, is rather like a cross-bow on a stand, and fired heavy arrows well over three hundred yards. The string which drove the arrow was attached to two wooden arms which were bedded in two twisted skeins of gut. Gut is difficult and expensive to find, so we used rubber strands, but they still brought the arms forward with a tremendous whack when the string was released. The string is hauled back on a ratchet operated by a lever and fitted over the arrow, which lay in a trough projecting through the shield of the catapult. The weapon was extremely powerful and accurate, in fact we nearly found it too much so, when we discovered a solitary cow had wandered unknown to us into the ditch behind the point which we were aiming at on the rampart!

Against such weapons and the discipline of the Roman legion, the Britons could have little chance. Maiden Castle, in spite of its great defences, was taken. But the event, like the others before it, left its mark. Nineteen hundred years later the excavators came on the moving evidence of the fight, what Sir Mortimer calls the first British war cemetery.

Amongst the ashes of the huts burnt during the fighting in the eastern entrance were uncovered the bodies of twenty-three men and eleven women. On their bones, those of men and women alike, were the marks of the wounds which had caused their deaths. One skull had nine cuts in it.

Their graves also revealed something more. Though they had been buried in haste, and one can imagine the feelings of terror and dismay that must have prevailed at the time, some attempt had been made at the proper treatment of the dead. One, perhaps a notorious beer drinker, had a handled mug to accompany him on his last journey. Another had the remains of a joint of lamb.

We were able to show these relics in the studio, as well as photographs of the graves, where they were found. But perhaps most striking of all was the vertebra of a victim with an arrow-head catapulted into it. Look at that in the Dorchester Museum, and it is not hard to imagine the siege and capture of Maiden Castle (Pl. 63).

The hill-top had yet to see a small Roman Temple and a Saxon burial. Then it was left to the cropping sheep and the larks. The visitor, the film cameraman, and even the archaeologist interrupt them only momentarily. Grass covers the scars of history, and the great banks and ditches alone remain, evidence of two thousand years of event and occupation.

CHAPTER XII

THE PEAT BOG
MURDER MYSTERY

A FEW YEARS AGO some peat-cutters working in the Tollund peat bog in Denmark reported to the police that they had uncovered the dead body of a man. The bog where the body was found was in a small, lonely valley in a desolate heather-clad area, and the police at once suspected that it might be connected with a recent unsolved murder. But further investigation soon yielded some very remarkable facts. The body turned out to have been under 8 feet of undisturbed peat, which meant it could be no recent murder. This was further confirmed by a local archaeologist who was summoned to the scene by the police. He believed the body to be prehistoric.

The man was naked except for a leather belt and cap, and the cause of his death was clearly visible, a leather noose drawn tightly round his neck. Thanks to the tannic acid in the peat, which had stopped the normal decaying action of the bacteria, his body was extremely well preserved, and it was at once taken with great care to the National Museum at Copenhagen for further study (Pl. 66).

The dating was helped by the fact that a number of other bodies, none of them so intact, have been found in northern Europe in similar circumstances. This, together with the depth of the peat, seemed to indicate that the body dated from the Iron Age and was about two thousand years old.

To preserve the whole body was considered both too expensive and too difficult in the present state of knowledge, so the head and the feet were kept, while the rest was handed over to the Laboratory of the National Museum at Copenhagen for research and examination. The head meanwhile was submitted to eighteen months' treatment and is now permanently preserved for posterity.

There could hardly have been a better subject for a spectacular start to a television series. To show millions of people this extraordinary relic

G

and discuss the problem of how and why he met his death would surely interest almost everybody. So Dr Daniel and I found ourselves in Copenhagen, where the head had been brought from its normal place in the Silkeborg museum, with the privilege of actually handling and examining it.

It is a quite remarkable experience to see for the first time this almost undamaged face from the past. In preservation the head has shrunk slightly from its original size and the weight of the peat has crushed in and slightly twisted the left side of the face, but otherwise it is entirely normal. In colour it is black, with the texture of hard, polished leather. The two most remarkable features are the eyes and the beard. Some men did shave at that time as Bronze and Iron Age razors have frequently been found in Scandinavia, but his beard must have continued to grow for some time after his death, because above the surface of the skin there is a fine stubble clearly visible. The eyes are shut, but the humour in the wrinkles at the corners and the serenity of his expression make him seem only separated from us by sleep, not two thousand years. Nor is it the face of a remote savage or barbarian. With its nobility and repose, it is a most haunting sight.

Filming the head presented a considerable problem. While the preservative process is now complete, the Copenhagen authorities were naturally anxious about whether the heat from the film lighting might not do some damage. They finally agreed to the filming this once on condition that our cameraman, Tubby Englander, used as little light as possible, and that copies of our film were given to the Danish Television Service and the Archives of the National Museum as the only film record permitted of Tollund Man.

For its first appearance in the programme I arranged the head on a turntable against an absolutely plain background, with cap towards the camera. Dr Daniel told the story of the finding of the body and then with the words, 'more than any other relic, Tollund Man brings us face to face with the past', we went over to the shot of the head, which slowly turned in absolute silence towards the camera to reveal the extraordinary 2,000-year-old countenance.

The noose of finely-plaited leather, which had caused his death, was drawn tightly into the folds of his neck. If the police of today escaped an awkward case through his antiquity, archaeologists are left with an even more difficult problem. Why was he put to death? This was the mystery I set Dr Daniel and Sir Mortimer Wheeler to solve in the programme. That a suicide by hanging should be cut down and carefully placed in the middle of a bog is hardly probable. Murder, too, seems to come in the same category, for hanging is not the easiest method to choose, and there were no signs of violence on the body.

They considered that three possible reasons were left. He was hanged for some crime, he was executed as a prisoner of war, or he was offered as a sacrifice to the gods. We know that in contemporary North German tribes hanging was an honourable method of execution. Criminals were more often drowned in the bogs. Tollund Man's distinction and serenity of face, too, seem to argue against his being a criminal. That he was an executed prisoner of war is arguable from some points of view. The habits of the Gauls with prisoners of war, as described by Julius Caesar, would certainly bear this idea out. There is also a scene shown on the famous Gundestrup bowl, a silver sacrificial vessel also found in a Danish bog which I will say more about, of a captive apparently having his throat cut (Pl. 65). On the other hand, one might expect to find in that case either other bodies or the weapons of a beaten enemy. Weapons broken after a battle and deposited in bogs as a thank-offering to the gods for victory have been found in considerable numbers in Denmark.

That makes the final reason the most likely to most authorities. It was a common practice in prehistoric Scandinavia to throw offerings to the gods into the many lakes or bogs, and hanging was considered a sacred death. The serenity of his expression, slight evidence though it is, would fit in with this idea. The Iron Age was a poor period in Denmark. Living conditions were hard, and food was short, as the contents of Tollund Man's stomach show. His death occurred in winter. Perhaps then, he went to his death, 2,000 years ago, sustained by the thought of the renewal of the crops his life would win from the gods, little knowing that the face he put on this hard decision would survive for us as one of the most striking revelations and enigmas that have come out of the past. Sir Mortimer, however, not uncharacteristically, did not agree with the majority about this. He preferred the criminal theory, offence unspecified, and it would need a bold and well-informed man to say categorically that he was wrong.

While we can only guess the reason for his death, and his cap and belt tell us little, Tollund Man does provide a good deal of information about a rather surprising subject, the food in Iron Age Denmark. When his body was examined at the Copenhagen Museum no sign of sickness or damage was found other than that caused by the hanging. The contents of his stomach, as described in the Report of the National Museum of Copenhagen, were therefore an accurate record of his last meal. This, incidentally, from the stage of digestion it had reached, seems to have been eaten between twelve and twenty-four hours before his death.

As a guide to a prehistoric diet, it is correct as to content, but provides only certain clues as to how food might have been cooked then. The first and most striking point is that his stomach held no traces whatsoever of meat. Surprising as it may seem, this agrees with other evidence from the time. Hunting weapons are hardly ever found in the graves and remains of houses of this period, and there are few bones in the refuse heaps. The game that had varied the diet of the Late Stone Age inhabitants of Lough Gur did not exist here, and a living had to be got almost entirely from vegetables and crops. Domestic animals, sheep, cattle, goats, and pigs were kept as well, but presumably, from the rarity of their remains, they were not as prolific as those of the builders of the West Kennet long barrow and were much too precious to kill off for meat, except on special occasions.

Tollund Man's last meal, then, was vegetable, and with the aid of the microscope it has been possible to identify the remains of nearly all the grains and seeds of which it consisted.

First of all there was barley. Barley was the most important cereal at this time, and it was not until Viking times that wheat was imported from England as a luxury for chiefs.

Then there was linseed, the seed of flax. There is one slight difficulty about eating this in large quantities. It has a well-known laxative effect. However, you can overcome this by soaking the seeds in water for some time, or boiling and draining them carefully. This presumably they did, for there is no reason to suppose that Tollund man's stomach was very much stronger than ours.

Another seed rich in oil that was also present in good quantities was camelina, one of the mustard family. This was probably cultivated along with the flax. The oil content of the two of them make them valuable and nourishing food.

Then there were the seeds of the pale persicaria, whose straggly leaves and long, fluffy, pink flowers are very common on waste ground and bombed sites. These seeds from this first group are very frequently found on other Iron Age sites, so it looks as though they were either specially cultivated or at least were the main object of seed-gathering expeditions.

The remaining seeds were only present in very small quantities, so they were probably either just picked accidentally or if the seed-gatherers happened to come across them. There were corn spurrey, white goosefoot, a wild brother of the turnip, and wild pansy, or heartsease.

There was one puzzling ingredient, some shreds of sphagnum moss. He could hardly have eaten this deliberately, and one ingenious scientist did suggest that it might have been forced down his throat after death.

But more probably he had had a drink from a bog-pool and the moss had got swilled down with it. With it, too, or perhaps from the store-houses where the seeds were kept, came the teaspoonful of fine sand which was also present.

So much can be said for certain. How the ingredients were cooked is more a matter of deduction. The seeds were not roasted or baked, because none of them showed any signs of having been burnt or scorched. That means they cannot have been made into bread, which is not known to have appeared in this part of the world before A.D. 400. The surviving first specimen from that date was in the shape of a charred bun made from barley and gravel. The next example, four hundred years later, was made from coarsely ground peas and spruce bark, so perhaps Tollund man's lack of bread was not such a deprivation as it would be to us. He could hardly have eaten all these seeds raw, which means they must have been boiled into a sort of soup or gruel. It is not even necessary to support this theory with arguments about the continuing popularity of porridge in Norway. Clay pots dating from this period have been found with crusts sticking to them that must have come from a form of porridge.

In the programme on Tollund man, I thought it would be interesting to try to cook this dish, and see what it was like. Finding the correct seeds was a problem, but eventually with the help of Kew, the seed research station at Cambridge, and a shop specializing in bird food, we managed to collect them all. Having got Doctor White and Miss Walley of the Dietetics Department of London University to experiment with the prescribed ingredients, we then cooked them all together and Noëlle Middleton dished it out for Dr Daniel and Sir Mortimer Wheeler to try. By boiling the seeds slowly together in a good quantity of water, after duly soaking the linseed and camelina seeds first, a rather oily porridge emerged. The most unattractive part of this was its colour, a greyish-purple flecked with the orange and black of the smaller seeds, but the actual taste, though unexciting, was quite reasonable. An indignant Dane wrote denying that his ancestors could possibly have lived on such dis-gusting food, after Sir Mortimer's cheerful observation that 'Tollund man probably committed suicide to escape his wife's cooking'. But, though not very appetizing, it would make a perfectly edible and sus-taining diet. The mash that many farm-horses are fed on is not very different, and Pliny describes the diet of Greek and Roman peasants as consisting of a gruel made of 20 pounds of barley, 3 pounds of linseed, half a pound of coriander seed and some salt, which is nearly enough the same.

Salt would improve the Tollund gruel, and would not have left any traces, but it was comparatively rare, being obtained by boiling sea-water or burning sea-weed. Honey is another possible accompaniment, but milk is unlikely. This was hardly ever drunk in its natural state. It was generally made into cream cheese, or butter, which was made from sour cream heavily salted and stored underground for some time. Incidentally, one of the differences between the Romans and the barbarians beyond the northern borders of the Empire at this time was that the Romans made cheese by adding rennet, whereas the Iron Age Scandinavians let the milk go sour and become cream cheese.

Finally, we can complete his possible menu with some drink. Pytheas, the Greek explorer, who travelled to Denmark about 325 B.C., describes the inhabitants as drinking beer and mead. Rather more exotic were the remains in the bottom of a bucket found in a Bronze Age grave, a thousand to fifteen hundred years earlier than Tollund man. The chemists decided these were the crystallized dregs of a cranberry wine flavoured with honey and bog myrtle.

But while Tollund man is perhaps the most fascinating treasure from the past yielded up by the Danish bogs, archaeologists have to thank the prehistoric habit of throwing offerings there for several other remarkable finds shown to me by Dr Brønsted, the Director of the Copenhagen Museum. The Gundestrup Bowl I have already mentioned. This was made of silver and found in pieces. Restored, it is about 3 feet in diameter and 15 inches high, covered inside and out with scenes done in an extraordinarily simple but skilled and powerful style. Besides the prisoner of war having his throat cut over a sacrificial vessel, which probably explains the use of this bowl, there are cavalrymen in plus-fours, dancing girls, a man wrestling with a lion, strange gods, an extraordinary dachshund-like creature with a head at each end, winged horses, and an eastern king with reindeer horns on his head, sitting cross-legged, holding a torque in one hand and a serpent by the neck in the other. Some authorities see an Eastern influence in this and think the bowl must have been made in Scythia, just north of the Black Sea, like the Princess of Vix's diadem, and found its way to Denmark as plunder or tribute. It is impossible to interpret all the scenes, but anyone can enjoy the artist's idea of an elephant. He had obviously only heard of them, not seen them, so he made them look like horses with long dangling noses. While the effect which the Etruscans had on the Celts never reached Scandinavia, and Tollund man's life was backward compared with that of the later inhabitants of Maiden Castle, this bowl does show that some of the ferment of civilization had got to this area.

Other remarkable finds are the Trundholm sun-chariot and the Djebjerg cart. The Trundholm sun-chariot is a small bronze model of a horse pulling a chariot with a flat disc, covered with gold, about 4 inches in diameter standing up in it. Clearly the sun was conceived as being pulled across the heavens by his steeds, and this was the image or some part of the worship of the sun god. Nothing else quite like this has ever been found, so it is unique evidence of the religion of Bronze Age man.

The Djebjerg cart has been reconstructed out of the remains of two that were found together in a bog. It has four wheels, a long shaft, and is about 4 feet high, 7 feet long, and 4 feet wide. Most of it is covered with finely worked decorative bronze. The rims of the wheels are made of a single piece of wood bent round and covered with an iron tyre. An engraved drawing on a piece of Iron Age pottery from Hungary shows a scene that may explain the use of this cart. In the drawing, the cremated remains of a chief in a large pottery urn are being drawn along, presumably to a burial place, on a four-wheeled cart pulled by two horses, while the chief's charger is led along ahead. Once again, the parallel with the chariot-burial of Vix strikes one.

You can see the Trundholm chariot and the Djebjerg cart at Copenhagen in the National Museum, together with the many other objects that have also been found in the prolific Danish bogs—weapons, armour, boats, figures, and the famous long, curling trumpets, the Lurs, whose deep notes we use for the closing signature tune of our 'Buried Treasure' programmes. But the most moving thing of all in his Silkeborg home is undoubtedly Tollund man.

I have strong personal reasons for thinking this. His face helped to launch 'Buried Treasure' successfully. As far as one can tell, these programmes have given pleasure and interest to a considerable number of people; for me, they have provided the fascinating experience of seeing and learning about the sites described in this book at first hand. But on any count, I think Tollund man is remarkable.

If his date was just A.D. rather than B.C., which is quite possible, he could by travelling south have met Christianity, the philosophy of Plato and Aristotle, Roman law, town planning, central heating, mass entertainment, and many other things that are an essential part of our life today. Yet his own life would not have seemed very strange to the earliest *Homo sapiens*. The crops he lived off would have been a novelty, but in many ways his was a poorer and more straitened existence than that of the cave-painting hunters of the old Stone Age. If his death was that of a sacrifice to fertility it would have been entirely comprehensible to the early Neolithic farmers, whose similar ideas left us their great stone tombs and temples. Who knows, it might not even have seemed very odd to Pekin man, who added to his strength by eating the brains of his enemies.

Yet to us this extraordinary face, so remarkably poised between the remotest past and the present, is essentially that of a fellow creature. It is no way strange, alien, or barbarian. More than most things, it brings the past alive to our imaginations, and reminds us how close to us and how much a part of us it is. To study it is to know ourselves better, and if we know clearly whence we came, there is more chance we may see a little less dimly where we are going.

Bibliography

The list below consists of the main literary sources for the material used in the programmes and also of some suggestions for further reading.

CHAPTER I

OAKLEY, K. P., three articles in *The Archaeological News Letter*, Vol. 5 No. 6, Oct.-Nov. 1954, pp.100–1; Vol. 5 No. 7, Dec. 1954, pp. 121–5; Vol. 5 No. 9, Feb. 1955, pp.163–4.

OAKLEY, K. P. and WEINER, J., 'Piltdown Man', *American Scientist*, Vol. 43 No. 4, Oct. 1955, pp. 573–83.

WEINER, J., *The Piltdown Forgery*, Oxford University Press, 1955.

Bulletin of the British Museum (Natural History), 'Further contributions to the solution of the Piltdown problem.' Nov. 1953.

CHAPTER II

COON, Carleton, *The History of Man*, Cape, 1955.

LEAKEY, L. S. B., *Adam's Ancestors*, Methuen, 1953.

OAKLEY, K. P., *Man, the Toolmaker*, British Museum (Natural History), 3rd edition, 1956.

SINGER, C., HOLMYARD, E. J. and HALL, A. R. (edited by), *The History of Technology*, Vol. I, Oxford University Press, 1954.

CHAPTER III

BANDI, Maringer and Hans-George, *Art in the Ice Age*, Allen & Unwin, 1953.

BREUIL, Abbé H. and WINDELS, F., *Four Hundred Centuries of Cave Art*, Centre of Prehistoric Studies and Documentation at Montignac, Dordogne, 1952.

BRODRICK, A. H., *Prehistoric Painting*, Avalon Press, 1948.

DANIEL, Glyn, *Lascaux and Carnac*, Lutterworth Press, 1955.

WINDELS, F., *The Lascaux Cave Paintings*, Faber, 1949.

CHAPTER IV

CLARK, Grahame, *From Savagery to Civilization*, Cobbett Press, 1940.
      The Mesolithic Age in Britain, Cambridge University Press, 1932.
      Prehistoric Europe: the Economic Basis, Methuen, 1952.

SINGER, C., HOLMYARD, E. J., and HALL, A. R. (edited by), *A History of Technology*, Vol. 1, Oxford University Press, 1954.

CHAPTER V

EVANS, John D., 'The Prehistoric Culture-Sequence in the Maltese Archipelago,' in *Proceedings of the Prehistoric Society*, Pt. I, 1953.

EVANS, John D., *Malta*, Thames & Hudson, 1957.

CHAPTER VI

DANIEL, Glyn, *The Prehistoric Chamber Tombs of England and Wales*, Cambridge University Press, 1950.

Ó RIÓRDAÍN, Séan, P., *Antiques of the Irish Countryside*, Methuen, 1953.
'Lough Gur Excavations—Neolithic and Bronze Age Houses on Knockadoon', in *Proceedings of the Royal Irish Academy*, Vol. 56, Section C., 1954.

PIGGOTT, Stuart, *The Neolithic Cultures of the British Isles*, Cambridge University Press, 1954.

POWELL, T. G. E. and DANIEL, G. E., *Barclodiad y Gawres*, Liverpool University Press, 1956.

WHEELER, Sir Mortimer, *Archaeology from the Earth*, Oxford University Press, 1956.

CHAPTER VII

CLARK, Grahame, *Prehistoric England*, Batsford, 1940.

HAWKES, J. and C., *Prehistoric Britain*, Chatto and Windus, 1947.

PIGGOTT, Stuart, *The Neolithic Cultures of the British Isles*, Cambridge University Press, 1954.

CHAPTER VIII

ATKINSON, R., *Stonehenge*, Hamish Hamilton, 1956.

PIGGOTT, Stuart, 'Stonehenge Reviewed', in *Aspects of Archaeology in Britain and Beyond*, ed. W. F. Grimes, H. W. Edwards, 1951.

A forthcoming publication that will include the results of the latest work on Stonehenge:
PIGGOTT, Stuart and HAWKES, C., *Victoria County History of Wiltshire*, Vol. I.

CHAPTER IX

JOHNSTONE, M. A., *Etruria Past and Present*, Methuen, 1930.

LAWRENCE, D. H., *Etruscan Places*, Heinemann (Phoenix edition), 1956.

NEPPI MODONA, A., *A Guide to Etruscan Antiquities*, Olschki, Florence 1954.

PALLOTTINO, M., *Etruscan Painting*, Skira, Geneva, 1952.
The Etruscans, Pelican Books, 1955
and HURLIMANN, M., *Art of the Etruscans*, Thames and Hudson, 1955.

RANDALL-McIVER, D., *The Etruscans*, Oxford University Press, 1924.

VON CLES-REDIN, S., *The Buried People*, Hart-Davies, 1955.

CHAPTER X

JOFFROY, R., *Le Trésor de Vix*, Presses Universitaires de France, 1954.

CHAPTER XI

HAWKES, J. and C., *Prehistoric Britain*, Chatto & Windus, 1947.
WHEELER, Sir Mortimer, *Maiden Castle*, Society of Antiquaries of London, 1943.

CHAPTER XII

Aarböger for Nordisk Oldkyndighed, Copenhagen, 1954.
SHETELIG, H., and FALK, H., *Scandinavian Archaeology* (trans. E. V. Gordon),
    Oxford University Press, 1937.

GENERAL ARCHAEOLOGY

CRAWFORD, O. G. S., *Archaeology in the Field*, Phoenix House, revised edition,
    1954.
KENYON, Kathleen, *Beginning in Archaeology*, Phoenix House, revised edition, 1953.

Index

Acheulian culture, 22
Agriculture and civilization, 33, 34, 37–8, 39, 41
Altamira cave paintings, 26–7
Atkinson, Richard, 58, 59, 62, 66, 67, 68, 70, 71
Australopithecus, 21, 22

Barclodiad y Gawres, 50
Beaker culture, 61–2, 72, 91
Belgae, The, 95
Breuil, Abbé Henri, 27, 28, 29
Brittany, 93–4
Brønsted, Dr, 102
Bronze Age, 51, 61, 63, 72, 75, 91, 102, 103
Burial customs, 40, 41, 45, 46, 51, 53, 61, 78, 91, 96, 103. *See also* Graves
Burkitt, Miles, 29, 30

Cannibalism, 91
Carbon 14 dating, 28
Catapult, Roman, 95–6
Cave art:
    Altamira, 26–7
    Brandberg, 27–8
    date of, 28
    La Mouthe, 27
    Lascaux, 25, 29, 31
    purpose of, 31, 32
    technique, 29–30
Châtillon-sur-Seine, 84
Childe, Gordon, 38
Chimaera, The, 82
Cliff castles, 93–4
Coon, Professor Carleton, 18
Copenhagen, National Museum, 97, 98, 102, 103
Cornwall, 94

Cro-Magnon man, 12, 23–4
Culture, a, defined, 22

Daniel, Dr Glyn, 9, 26, 28, 29, 50, 51, 74, 98
Dawson, Charles, 11, 12, 15, 16, 17
Denmark, 97-103
Djebjerg cart, 103

Etruscans, 73–83, 89
    art and metalwork, 73, 76, 79–80, 82, 87
    character, 73–4, 77
    cities, 75–6, 79
    origins, 75
    religion, 80–1
    ships, 77
    social organization, 80
    tombs, 73, 78–9
Evans, Professor John, 42, 44, 45, 46, 48–9, 50

Fluorine test, 13

Gigantija, 43–4
Gozo, 43–4
Grange stone circle, 54
Graves and tombs:
    Etruscan, 73, 78–9
    gallery, 52, 54
    at Jericho, 36
    long barrow, 58–9, 62, 63–4
    at Maiden Castle, 91, 96
    passage, 50, 52–3
    at Vix, 85–6, 87
Gundestrup bowl, 99, 102